Raniero Cantalamessa

The Eucharist
Our Sanctification

Translated by Frances Lonergan Villa

Revised Edition

A Liturgical Press Book

THE LITURGICAL PRESS
Collegeville, Minnesota

Cover design by Ann Blattner.
Cover icon: *The Last Supper* (11th century),
State Museum for Russian Art, Kiev.

Published originally in Italian under the title *L'Eucaristia nostra santificazione* by Editrice Àncora Milano in 1983.

9

Library of Congress Cataloging-in-Publication Data

Cantalamessa, Raniero.
    [Eucaristia nostra santificazione. English]
    The Eucharist, our sanctification / Raniero Cantalamessa ;
translated by Frances Lonergan Villa.
      p.   cm.
    ISBN 0-8146-2075-2
    1. Lord's Supper.   2. Sanctification.   3. Sacraments—Catholic
Church.   4. Catholic Church—Doctrines.   I. Title.
BX2215.2.C2613   1993
234'.163—dc20   92-40433
                                                     CIP

Contents

Chapter One

"Christ Our Passover Has Been Immolated"

The Eucharist in the History of Salvation

In this first chapter we shall consider the mystery of the Last Supper against the background of the whole history of salvation. God revealed himself to us in a historical context which, because of its content and intention, is called the "history of salvation." Within the framework of world history, made up of events that are visible and can be recorded, another history unfolds. Unlike human history, this does not deal with wars, peace or people's inventions but with God's "inventions," the *mirabilia Dei,* the wonderful and benevolent interventions of God. Everything God does outside himself (*ad extra*) from the creation right up to the end of the world, is part of this history. The coming of Jesus in the incarnation brings about a sudden upsurge as when a river arrives at a lock and then flows on higher up. Everything Jesus did during his life is part of the history of salvation, even his silence and everyday life in Nazareth! His time is the "heart of time" and the "fullness of time." But the history of salvation goes on after him and we are part of it. The life of every Christian is a short history of salvation from baptism to death; it is the microcosm of salvation, whereas what takes place from creation to the parousia is the macrocosm. The final coming of Christ will bring about another decisive leap in this long history: this time a leap from history to what lies beyond history, from time to eternity; from hope to possessing and from faith to glory.

We are, therefore, living in the fullness of time which began with the incarnation, at a point situated between "already" and "not yet." If we picture the history of salvation as a long line in time, we can indicate the "already" with a continuous line that stretches right up to the present day, and the "not yet," what we are waiting for to happen, with a dotted line which may end at any point, as this very night the Lord might return.

The question now is what place the Eucharist has in the history of salvation. Where should we place it along the line? And the answer is that it has no particular place — it is the whole thing. The Eucharist is coextensive with the history of salvation: the entire history of salvation is present in the Eucharist and the Eucharist is present in the entire history of salvation. Just as on a clear morning the whole sky is reflected in a dewdrop on a bush so the Eucharist reflects the whole of the history of salvation.

The Eucharist, however, is present in this history in three different ways at distinct times, or stages: it is present in the Old Testament as a *figure,* in the New Testament as an *event,* and in our time, the time of the Church, as a *sacrament.* The figure anticipates and prepares the event, the sacrament "prolongs" the event and actualizes it.

1. *Figures and foreshadowings of the Eucharist in the Old Testament*

As I have just said, the Eucharist is present in the Old Testament as a "figure." The entire Old Testament was a preparation of the Lord's Supper. "A man once gave a great banquet": "Who was this man," St. Augustine asked, "if not Jesus Christ, God and man's mediator?" "At the time for the banquet he sent his servant to say to those who had been invited, 'Come, for all is now ready' " (Luke 14:16ff.): "who had been invited if not those who had been called by the prophets? Since when they themselves had been sent, the prophets invited others to Christ's supper. They had been sent to the people of Israel; many times they were sent and many times they invited others so that they might come to the supper at the right time."[1]

The expectation of the hour of the supper was kept alive not only by the prophets' words but also through figures or "types," and, that is, through some signs or rites that were the visible preparation, almost an "outline" of Christ's supper.

One of these figures, recalled by Jesus himself, was the manna (cf. Exod 16:4ff.; John 6:31ff.). Another was the sacrifice of Melchizedech who offered bread and wine (cf. Gen 14:18; Ps 110:4; Heb 7:1ff.). The sacrifice of Isaac was another. In the

"Lauda Sion," composed by St. Thomas Aquinas for the feast of "Corpus Domini," we sing: "In old types foresignified: In the manna heaven-supplied, In Isaac and the paschal Lamb."

Of all these figures of the Eucharist there is one that is more than a "figure": the Passover! From it the Eucharist takes its name and its aspect of the Lord's Supper. It is in reference to it that Jesus is called the "Lamb of God." From the very night of the Exodus out of Egypt, God contemplated the Eucharist and thought of giving us the true lamb. God says: "When I see the blood, I will pass over you" (Exod 12:13), that is to say, I shall save you and not destroy you. At this point, the Fathers of the Church wondered what the Lord saw over the Jews' houses that was so precious to make him "pass over" and tell his angel not to destroy them, and their answer was: he saw the Blood of Christ, he saw the Eucharist! One of the earliest Passover texts of the Church says: "O new and inexpressible mystery! The slaying of the lamb became the salvation of Israel, the death of the lamb became life for the people and its blood frightened the angel (cf. Exod 12:23). Angel, answer me: What was it that filled you with fear: the slaying of the lamb or the Lord's life? The lamb's death or the Lord's life? The lamb's blood or the Lord's Spirit? What you feared is clear: you saw the Lord's mystery fulfilled in the lamb, the Lord's life in the slaying of the lamb, the figure of the Lord in the lamb's death and for this you did not destroy Israel."[2] "What must the power of the reality be (i.e., the Christian Passover), if a simple figure of it caused salvation?"[3] It was due to their efficacy as figures of the Eucharist that St. Thomas called the rituals of the Old Testament "the sacraments of the old Law."[4]

In Jesus's time the Jewish Passover took place in two stages: the first consisted of the slaying of the lamb and this took place in the Temple of Jerusalem on the afternoon of the 14 Nisan; the second stage was the eating of the victim during the Passover supper in each family on the night following the 14 Nisan. During the liturgy of the supper, the head of the family, vested with priestly dignity for the occasion, would explain the significance of the ritual, giving his children an outline of God's wonderful intervention in his people's history. In Jesus's time the Passover had become the "memorial" not only of the Exodus out of Egypt, but also of all the other interventions God made in the history of Israel. The Passover was the memorial and anniversary of the most important four nights in the world: the night of creation when the light shone in the darkness, the night of Abraham's sacrifice of Isaac, the night of the Exodus out of Egypt and the night, still to come, of the coming of the Messiah.[5]

The Jewish Passover was, therefore, a *memorial* (cf. Exod 12:14) and it was a *waiting,* too. The disaster was that when the Messiah did come, he was not accepted. They "did what they wanted with him" and killed him precisely during a Passover feast. But in killing him, they fulfilled the figure and what had been awaited, that is, the immolation of the true Lamb of God. As usual, people swarmed into Jerusalem in those days to celebrate the Passover but none of them knew that in one of the "upper rooms" of the city the event that had been awaited for centuries was being fulfilled. When Jesus took bread and gave thanks, he broke it and gave it to his disciples saying, "This is my body which is given for you. Do this in remembrance of me" (Luke 22:19), the word "remembrance," "memory" must have immediately recalled the same word in Exodus and made them think he was instituting a new Passover. In fact, the ancient memorial remains but its content has changed or, better still, it has been fulfilled. From now on the Passover will be in remembrance of another immolation and another passage. "O blessed night, in which the night of Egypt was fulfilled. Our Lord consumed the little Passover and became himself the great Passover; the Passover substituted the Passover, the feast substituted the feast. Behold the Passover that passes and the Passover that doesn't pass; behold the figure and its fulfillment."[6]

2. *The Eucharist as an event*

At this point we are in the fullness of time: the Eucharist is no longer present simply as a figure, it has become a reality. The ancient Passover hasn't been destroyed or forgotten, it has just been superimposed by another infinitely more important one which surpasses it while confirming it. The wonderful news is enclosed in St. Paul's exclamation: "Christ, our paschal lamb, has been sacrificed!" (1 Cor 5:7). That's why the Eucharist can be called "the old and new mystery: old because of the prefiguration, new because of its fulfillment."[7]

What, precisely, was the event that established the Eucharist and brought the new Passover into existence? The Gospels answer this question in two different, yet complementary, ways which, together, give us a wider view of the mystery like something seen from two different angles. The Jewish Passover, as we have seen, took place at two different times and in two different places: the immolation in the Temple and the supper in the people's homes. John the evangelist gives more attention to the immolation. For him the Christian Passover — and therefore the Eucharist — was instituted on the cross, at the moment in which Jesus, the true Lamb of God, was immolated. His Gospel contains a remarkable synchronism. On the one hand he constantly emphasizes the approach of the Jewish Passover ("Six days before the Passover," "Now before the feast of the Passover," "it was the day of the Passover"), and on the other hand, he stresses that Jesus's hour was near, the hour of his "glorification" which was the hour of his death. There is, therefore, a "temporal" approach — a precise day and time — and a "spatial" approach — towards Jerusalem — until the afternoon of the 14 Nisan, when time and space converge on Calvary, precisely at the moment when the immolation of the Passover lambs was due to start in the Temple. In order to lay further stress on this coincidence, John underlines the fact that of Jesus on the Cross "not a bone was broken" (John 19:36) as the ordinance prescribed for the Passover victim (cf. Exod 12:46). It is as if at that moment the evangelist, pointing to Jesus on the Cross, solemnly proclaimed to the world: "Behold the Lamb of God, who takes away the sin of the world!" (John 1:29).

All three Synoptic evangelists deal with the moment of the supper. For them, it was at the supper and precisely when the Eucharist was instituted, that the passage from the old to the new Passover took place. They give great importance to the preparation of the Last Passover Supper celebrated by Jesus before his death: "Where is the guest room, where I am to eat the Passover with my disciples?" (Luke 22:11). It could be said that in the Synoptics the Supper already anticipates and contains the Passover event of the immolation of Christ, just as in the prophets symbolic action sometimes anticipates the announced event. Symbolic action, or a prophetic gesture — such as Jeremiah breaking the potter's vessel (19:1ff.), or Ezechiel lying on his side (4:4ff.) — is not a simple visual aid to reinforce the proclamation; it is "a

9

creative prefiguration of the coming event which was to take place immediately after. As soon as the prophet, even if only through the limited means of signs, inserts the future in history, the future itself becomes present and therefore the prophet's sign is nothing but a sublime form of prophetic speech" (G. von Rad). "Prophetic signs are a concrete realization of God's word and they are events that anticipate the history that has been foretold by God's Word" (W. Zimmerli).

In this light, the breaking of the bread and the institution of the Eucharist by Jesus at the Last Supper was the supreme symbolic and prophetic action in the history of salvation. It follows the line of the symbolic actions of the prophets even if it is as superior to them as the words of Jesus are to those of the prophets and as the person of Jesus is to that of the prophets. In instituting the Eucharist, Jesus prophetically announced and sacramentally anticipated what was to come soon after — his death and resurrection — thereby already inserting the future in history. The preaching of Jesus announces God's kingdom that was to come; the institution of the Eucharist is the prophetic action that anticipates the fulfillment of this announcement which was to become a fact at the death-resurrection of Christ. The Fathers (especially the Syrian Fathers) so deeply felt the realism of Christ's gesture that they counted the "three days" Jesus spent in death from the moment when, in the cenacle, "he broke his body for his disciples" and not from the moment of his death on the Cross.[8] It is therefore the same fundamental event that the Synoptic Gospels present anticipated in the symbolic and sacramental action of the Eucharist and that John presents in its full and final manifestation on the cross.

John stresses the moment of the *real* immolation (the Cross), whereas the Synoptics stress the moment of the *mystical* immolation (the Supper). It is the same event seen from two different angles — the event of Christ's immolation. "At the supper," St. Ephrem wrote, "Jesus immolated himself; on the cross others immolated him"[9] and this was to show that no one could take his life if he didn't offer it freely as he had the power to lay it down and to take it again (cf. John 10:18).

The event that establishes, or institutes, the Eucharist is therefore the death and resurrection of Christ, his "laying down his life to take it again." We call it an event because it is a fact unique in both time and space, that took place once for all in the course

of history and can never again be repeated: "Christ has appeared
once for all at the end of the age to put away sin by the sacrifice
of himself" (Heb 9:26). But these are not just bare "facts"; there
is a reason, a why, behind them which constitutes, as it were, the
spirit of the facts, and that is, love. The Eucharist springs from
love; the reason for everything was that he loved us: "Christ loved
us and gave himself up for us, a fragrant offering and sacrifice
to God" (Eph 5:2). The Eucharist comes to us as the work and
gift of the whole Trinity; the entire Trinity is involved in the institution of the Eucharist: the Son who offers himself, the Father to whom he offers himself and the Holy Spirit through whom
he offers himself (cf. Heb 9:14).

The entire Trinity and not just Jesus takes part in the sacrifice
from which the Eucharist comes. This helps to set right any mistaken idea we might have about the Father. A certain modern
culture foolishly and sacrilegiously tries to transfer to God the
Father some prejudices used in psychoanalysis for the natural
father. Thus we imagine the Father, impassive in heaven, while
the Son dies upon the Cross, the Father who is even ready to accept the sacrifice of his Son's blood. A Father who takes but gives
nothing in return, who asks for the blood of his own Son as ransom, could not but inspire us with fear and dread. But this is a
mistaken representation. St. Paul tells us that the Father "did not
spare his own Son but gave him up for us all" (Rom 8:32). "For
us all": this is the key to it all. If the Father is pleased with the
Son's sacrifice it is because this gave him back his "children who
were scattered abroad" (cf. 11:52), and because it makes it possible for him to realize his dearest wish "that all men be saved"
(cf. 1 Tim 2:4). The Father loves Jesus with such boundless love
because he sacrificed himself for us; not, let us say, that he simply
sacrificed himself, but that he sacrificed himself for us. Besides,
God is always the God who desires "steadfast love and not sacrifice" (Hos 6:6); if he was pleased with his Son's sacrifice it was
because it allowed him to use mercy towards the world.

The Father is not, therefore, just the one who receives the Son's
sacrifice, he also gives his Son in sacrifice — he makes the sacrifice of giving us his Son! If, as St. Paul says, Jesus offered himself to God "for us," it is true that the sacrifice was made to God
but that God didn't benefit from it. We benefited and this is what
distinguishes Christian sacrifice from all others.

11

We could go on talking at length about the event of the Cross from which the Eucharist comes: we would never be able to say enough about the treasures it contains. There is enough energy in this event to make the salvation of history and the world depend on it. Referring to this moment, Jesus once said: "I came to cast fire upon the earth; and would that it were already kindled!" (Luke 12:49). Truly "all is accomplished" on the Cross; nothing greater can be thought of or done; it was there that every human and divine resource was consumed: all evil is conquered at its roots, salvation is obtained and every glory is given to the Trinity.

3. *The Eucharist as sacrament*

Let us now consider the third part of the history of salvation, the time of the Church in which we ourselves live. The Eucharist is present in it as a sacrament, in the signs of bread and wine, instituted by Jesus at the Last Supper with the words: "Do this in memory of me."

We must clearly understand the difference between the event we have so far described and the sacrament, the difference between history and liturgy. St. Augustine aids us in this. Christ — he says — died only once for us, the just one for sinners, the Lord for the servants. We know with certainty that this took place only once for all; and yet, the sacrament periodically renews it as if what history proclaims happened only once, was being repeated over and over again. Yet, the event and sacrament are not in contrast, almost as if the sacrament were false and the event true. In fact, the sacrament often renews (*renovat*) in the hearts of the faithful the celebration of what history states really took place only once. *History* reveals what happened once and how it happened, the *liturgy* keeps the past from being forgotten; not in the sense that it makes the past event happen again (*non faciendo*), but in the sense that it celebrates it (*sed celebrando*).[10]

It is an extremely delicate matter to define the link that exists between the unique sacrifice of the Cross and the Mass and it has always been one of the points of greatest dissent between Catholics and Protestants. As we have seen, Augustine uses two words: *renew* and *celebrate,* which are right, on condition that one is seen in the light of the other: the Mass renews the event of the Cross by celebrating it (not by reiterating it!) and celebrates it by renewing it (not just by recalling it!). The word that meets with the greatest ecumenical consent today, is, perhaps, the verb *represent* (also used by Paul VI in his encyclical "Mysterium fidei"), understood in its strongest sense, re-present or, make present again.[11]

According to history, therefore, there has only been the one Eucharist, realized by Jesus through his life and death; according to liturgy, instead, and thanks to the sacrament instituted by Jesus at the Last Supper, there are as many Eucharists as are celebrated and will be celebrated to the end of time. The event took place once only (*semel*), the sacrament takes place "every time" (*quotiescumque*).

It is due to the sacrament of the Eucharist that we mysteriously become contemporaries of the event; the event is present for us and we are present at the event. In the liturgy of the Passover night, the Jews of Jesus's time used to say: "In every generation, let each one see himself as the one that came out of Egypt that night."[12] Applied to us Christians, this text tells us that in every generation, each of us must see himself as one that stood beneath the Cross that day, with Mary and John. Yes, we were there; "everyone was born there" (Ps 87:4). Whenever I hear the Negro spiritual that says: "Were you there when they crucified the Lord?," I always answer in my heart: Yes, I was there!

The sacrament of the Eucharist doesn't make the event of the Cross present to us only; it would be too little; it makes it present above all to the Father. At every "breaking of the bread" when the priest breaks the host, it's as if the alabaster vase of Christ's humanity were being broken again, which is what happened on the Cross, and as if the perfume of his obedience were rising to touch the Father's heart again. Like Isaac smelling the smell of Jacob's garments and blessing him, and saying: "See, the smell of my son is as the smell of a field which the Lord has blessed" (Gen 27:27).

If we ask ourselves how it is that the event of the Cross is not ended and concluded in itself, like every other event in history, but is relevant even today, the ultimate answer is, the Holy Spirit! In his encyclical on the Holy Spirit, Pope Leo XIII states that "Christ fulfilled all his work, and especially his sacrifice, through the intervention of the Holy Spirit (*praesente Spiritu*)." During Mass, just before Communion, the priest prays and says: "Lord Jesus Christ, Son of the living God, by the will of the Father,

13 in the name of the Lord

and *the work of the Holy Spirit* your death brought life to the world. . . ." All of this is based on the words of Scripture which say that Christ, "through the eternal Spirit offered himself without blemish to God" (Heb 9:14). These words shed new light on the event of the Cross; it appears as a "spiritual" event, as the work of the Holy Spirit. It was the Holy Spirit, who is love, that stirred the depths of Christ's human heart to offer himself to the Father for us and that made him embrace the Cross.

The Holy Spirit is called the "eternal" Spirit in the verse just mentioned, where eternal means not destined to cease, like the sacrifices in the Old Testament, but to last forever. Thanks to the "eternal" Spirit, Jesus secured "eternal" redemption for us (cf. Heb 9:12). The sacrifice of the Cross as such ended precisely when Jesus, bowing his head, gave up his Spirit. But there was like a hidden flame in it, which once lit, could no longer be quenched, not even by death. Jesus of Nazareth did not stay with us "always" as such, he returned to the Father; instead, his Spirit remains with us "eternally." Jesus himself said so. The Jews objected: "We have heard from the Law that the Christ remains forever. How can you say that the Son of Man must be lifted up?" (John 12:34). Jesus replies indirectly shortly after when he says: "I will pray the Father, and he will give you another Counsellor, to be with you for ever" (John 14:16). Christ remains forever by giving his Spirit to his disciples to be with them forever.

This shows how the sacrifice of the Cross can, in a certain sense, still be going on. Like the whole life of Jesus, it is concluded and not concluded; it is momentary and lasting, momentary for history, lasting for the Spirit. The sacraments of the Church and especially the Eucharist, are made possible by the Spirit of Jesus living in the Church. This is the theological basis that gives rise to the importance of the epiclesis, and that is, the invoking of the Holy Spirit at the consecration of the offerings during Mass.

On the Cross, Jesus bowed his head and "gave up his Spirit" (cf. John 19:30); at every Mass, it's as if that last, unceasing breath of Jesus returned to hover over us, to move, as it were, the air and fill the congregation with Christ's presence. The wonder that took place at Elijah's prayer on Mount Carmel when the fire fell and consumed the burnt offering (cf. 1 Kgs 18, 38) is renewed each time in a spiritual and invisible way.

If we too celebrate our Mass, as Jesus did on the Cross, "in the company of the Holy Spirit," he will give new meaning and new light to our celebrations. He will really make us, as we ask in the canon of the Mass, "a living sacrifice pleasing to God."

NOTES

1. St. Augustine, *Sermon 112* (PL 38, 643).
2. St. Melito of Sardis, *Paschal Homily,* 31ff. (SCh 123, 76f.).
3. *Paschal Homily* of an Ancient Author (Ps.Hippolytus), 3 (SCh 27, 121).
4. St. Thomas Aquinas, *Theological Summa,* III, q. 60, a.2, 2.
5. Cf. *Targum of Exodus* 12, 42 (ed. R. Le Deaut, *La nuit pascale,* Rome 1963, 64ff.).
6. St. Ephrem, *Hymns on the Crucifixion,* 3, 2 (ed. Th. Lamy 1882, 656).
7. St. Melito of Sardis, *Paschal Homily,* 2f. (SCh 123, 60f.).
8. St. Ephrem, *Commentary on the Diatessaron,* 9, 4 (SCh 121, 333).
9. St. Ephrem, *Hymns on the Crucifixion,* 3, 1 (ed. Lamy, 655).
10. Cf. St. Augustine, *Sermon* 220 (PL 38, 1089).
11. Cf. Paul VI, Encycl. *Mysterium fidei* (AAS, 57, 1965, 753ff.).
12. *Pesachim,* X, 5.

Chapter Two

"This Is My Body Which Will Be Given Up For You"

The Eucharist makes the Church through Consecration

In chapter one we considered the Eucharist in the history of salvation where it is successively present as figure, as event and as sacrament. Here, and in the following chapters, we shall concentrate completely on the Eucharist-sacrament, and that is, on the Eucharist as it is today, in the Church. In this new light the Eucharist no longer appears to be at the center of the line that stretches from the Exodus to the second coming of Jesus, but at the center of a circle which ideally represents the Church, as she exists today, in all her reality. Actually, we could visualize all this in three concentric circles: a broad one representing the entire universe and inside this a smaller one which is the Church and finally, within this second circle a third still smaller one (even if it actually holds the entire universe), which is the Host. The Eucharist appears as the center and the sun, not only of the Church, but of the whole of humanity and the entire inanimate universe. The only difference is this: the Church has Jesus Christ at her center and *knows* it; the universe also has Jesus Christ at its center but *doesn't know* it!

The relation Eucharist-Church, which we are now going to consider, is not a static relation but a dynamic and active one. It is therefore not sufficient to say that the Eucharist *is* at the center of the Church, because actually, the Eucharist *makes* the Church! It builds it from within and weaves it round itself like a robe. It is said that two sacraments in particular "make" the Church: baptism and the Eucharist. But whereas baptism makes the Church grow quantitatively, as it were, in size and number, the Eucharist makes her grow qualitatively, in strength, because it transforms her ever more deeply into the image of Christ, her Head. The kingdom of heaven is like leaven which a woman took and hid in three

16

measures of meal (cf. Matt 13:33). The Eucharist too is like leaven; Jesus placed it in the mass of meal, his Church, so that it would "raise" it and make it ferment and become "bread," as he is! If the Church is the leaven of the world, the Eucharist is the leaven of the Church.

In various ways, or stages, the Eucharist "makes" the Church, it transforms her in Christ, by consecration, communion, contemplation and by imitation. We shall now reflect on the first of these ways or stages: the Eucharist makes the Church through consecration.

1. *"He broke the bread"*

In his Letter to the Romans, St. Paul wrote: "I appeal to you therefore, brethren, by the mercies of God, to present your bodies as a living sacrifice, holy and acceptable to God, which is your spiritual worship" (Rom 12:1). These words irresistibly recall the words Jesus spoke at the Last Supper: "Take, eat, this is my body which will be given for you." Therefore, when St. Paul exhorts us to offer our bodies as a sacrifice, it is as if he were saying: You also do what Jesus Christ did; you also be a Eucharist for God! He offered himself to God as a sacrifice of sweet odor; you offer yourselves as a living sacrifice acceptable to God!

It is Jesus himself, and not only the Apostle Paul, who exhorts us to do this. When, just after instituting the Eucharist, he said: "Do this in remembrance of me" (Luke 22:19), he didn't in fact just mean: Do exactly what I have done, repeat this same ritual. He was also saying: Do the essence of what I have done, offer your bodies as a sacrifice, as you have seen me do! "For I have given you an example, that you also should do as I have done" (John 13:15). But there is something even more pressing and heart-piercing in these words of Jesus. We are "his" body, "his" members (cf. 1 Cor 12:12ff.); so it's as if Jesus were saying to us: Allow me to offer the Father my own body; do not keep me from offering myself to the Father. I cannot offer myself completely to the Father while there is still one member of my body who refuses to offer himself with me! Therefore, complete what is still missing in my offer; make my joy perfect!

So let us look upon the moment of Eucharistic consecration in a new light, for we now know, as St. Augustine said, that "it is also our mystery that is celebrated on the altar."[1] I have said that to truly celebrate the Eucharist we should also "do" what Jesus did. But what did Jesus do that night? Above all, he accomplished an action: he broke bread. All the accounts of the institution of the Eucharist emphasize this action, so much so that the Eucharist was soon known as the "breaking of bread" (*fractio panis*). Yet, perhaps we haven't fully understood the meaning of his action. Why did Jesus break bread? Was it just to give a piece to each of his disciples? No, it wasn't! The action had, above all, a sacrificial meaning being consumed between Jesus and the Father. It didn't just signify sharing, but also immolation. The bread was himself; in breaking the bread, Jesus was "breaking" himself, in the sense Isaiah had said of the Servant of God: he was broken (*attritus*) for our transgressions (cf. Isa 53:5). A human creature, who is however the eternal Son of God, "breaks" himself before God and that is, he "obeys onto death," to reaffirm God's rights that have been violated by sin, to proclaim that God is God and that says everything.

It would be impossible to express in words the essence of the interior act that accompanies the action of breaking the bread. It might seem harsh and cruel whereas it is the most supreme act of love and tenderness that has ever been made, or can ever be made, on this earth. When, at the consecration, I hold the delicate host in my hands and repeat the words "He broke the bread . . .," I can sense something of the sentiments that filled the heart of Jesus at that moment: how he completely gave his human will to the Father, overcoming every resistance and repeating to himself these well-known words from Scripture: "Sacrifices and offerings thou hast not desired, but a body hast thou prepared for me; Lo, I have come to do thy will, O God" (cf. Heb 10:5-9). What Jesus gives his disciples to eat is the bread of his obedience and his love for the Father.

Then I understand that to "do" what Jesus did that night, I must, first of all, "break" myself and that is, lay before God all hardness, all rebellion towards him or towards others, crush my pride, submit and say "yes," fully, to all that God asks of me. I too must repeat the words: Lo, I have come to do thy will, O God! You don't want many things from me; you want me and I say "yes." To be Eucharist like Jesus signifies being totally abandoned to the Father's will.

2. *"Take this, all of you, and eat it"*

After breaking the bread and while he was giving it to his disciples, Jesus also uttered some words: "Take, eat, this is my body which is given for you" (Matt 26:26; Luke 22:19). I should like to tell my own experience on this; how, that is, I discovered that these words must become ours, just like the action of breaking the bread; in other words, how I discovered the ecclesial and personal dimension of the Eucharistic consecration.

Up to a certain time I used to live the moment of consecration at Mass by closing my eyes, bowing my head and trying to estrange myself from everything around me, and to identify myself with Jesus who, before his death, uttered these words in the cenacle: "Take, eat . . . ." Before the Vatican Council the liturgy itself encouraged this attitude, for the priest had to pronounce the words of consecration in a low voice in Latin, as he bent over the species. Then, one day, it struck me that this attitude didn't express the whole meaning of my participation in the consecration. The Jesus of the cenacle no longer exists! The risen Jesus exists now: the Jesus who was dead but now lives for evermore (cf. Rev 1:18). And this Jesus is the "total Christ," Head and body inseparably united. So, if it is this total Christ that says the words of consecration, I, too, say them with him. Within the great "I" of the Head, the small "I" of the body, which is the Church, is hidden. There is also my very small "I" and this says to those present: "Take this, all of you, and eat it: this is my body which will be given up for you!" What a mystery! Jesus has united me to himself in the most sublime and holiest action in history; in the only action really "worthy of God," worthy of his holiness and his majesty. Let the heavens marvel, the earth exult, the angels rejoice, the demons tremble: God has obtained what the universe was created for; his plan and wish have been fulfilled; nothing could prevent it, not even sin; his creature went back to him in a spontaneous gesture of love; he has given in sacrifice what he had received from God as a gift.

From the day I realized this, I no longer close my eyes at the moment of consecration but now that the Mass is celebrated facing the people I look at the brethren or, if there is no one present, I think of those I'm going to meet throughout the day and to whom I must dedicate my time, or, I think of the whole Church,

19

and addressing these, I say like Jesus: "Take this, all of you, and eat it: this is my body which I will give up for you."

Later some words of St. Augustine removed all doubt about this intuition, making me realize that it is the soundest of traditional doctrine, even if much attention is no longer paid to it. St. Augustine wrote: "The whole redeemed city, and that is the congregation of the saints, is offered to God as a universal sacrifice through the mediation of the high priest who offered himself for us in the form of servant so that we might become the body of so great a Head. The Church celebrates this mystery in the sacrament of the altar, well-known to the faithful, where the Church offers herself through what is being offered (*in ea re quam offert, ipsa offertur*)."[2]

Therefore, the Church, in the Eucharist, offers and is offered at the same time, and in each of her members. We cannot separate and divide the two things, as if the priest was offering and the rest of the Church, the laity, was being offered. Each member of the Church is simultaneously both priest and victim, while acknowledging, of course, the essential difference between the ministerial priesthood and the universal priesthood of all baptized persons. This is because Jesus, to whom we unite ourselves, is at the same time priest and victim, "without confusion, without division." "He is both priest and sacrifice before the Father for us: priest, precisely because he is victim."[3] This is the unique and unrepeatable characteristic of Christ's sacrifice which springs from the mystery of the hypostatic union of his human and divine nature. The consequence of this for personal sanctification is that the more a bishop or a priest shares in Christ's sacrifice the more he shares in his priesthood, the more perfectly he offers himself with Christ to the Father, the more he really offers Christ to the Father. On the altar the priest acts in the place of Christ the High Priest but also in the place of Christ the High Victim.

"Knowing," St. Gregory of Nazianzus wrote, "that no one is worthy of God's greatness, of the Victim and the Priest, if he hasn't first offered himself as a holy and acceptable oblation, (cf. Rom 12:1) and if he hasn't offered God a sacrifice of praise and a contrite spirit — the only sacrifice God asks for — how could I dare to offer him the external offering, that which represents the great mysteries, on the altar?"[4] The offering of the Body of Christ must be accompanied by the offering of one's own body.

This is, therefore, a clear and safe point of view on Eucharistic consecration. There are two bodies of Christ on the altar: his *real* body (the body "born of the Virgin Mary," risen and ascended into heaven) and his *mystic* body, the Church. Thus, his real body is *really* present and his mystic body is *mystically* present, "mystically" meaning in virtue of its inseparable union with the Head. There is no confusion and no division between the two presences which are distinct. The offering of ourselves and the Church would be nothing without Christ; it would be neither holy nor acceptable to God as we are only sinful creatures. But the offering of Jesus without that of the Church, his body, would not be sufficient. (It would not be sufficient for passive redemption, that is for receiving salvation, whereas it would be so for active redemption, that is for providing salvation). So true is this that the Church can exclaim with St. Paul: "In my flesh I complete what is lacking in Christ's afflictions" (cf. Col 1:24).

As there are two "offerings" and two "gifts" on the altar, that which is to become the Body and Blood of Christ (bread and wine) and that which is to become the mystical body of Christ, we also have two "epiklesis" in the Mass, or two invocations of the Holy Spirit. The first one says: "And so, Father, we bring you these gifts. We ask you to make them holy by the power of your Spirit, that they may become the body and blood of your Son our Lord Jesus Christ." In the second one, after the consecration, we pray: "Grant that we . . . may be filled with his Holy Spirit and become one body, one spirit in Christ. May he (the Holy Spirit) make us an everlasting gift to you."

Now we know how the Eucharist makes the Church: the Eucharist makes the Church by making the Church Eucharist! The Eucharist is not only the source and cause of the Church's holiness, it is also its model. Christian holiness must be realized according to the "form" of the Eucharist, it must be Eucharistic holiness. Christians cannot limit themselves to celebrating the Eucharist, they must be Eucharist with Jesus.

3. *"This is my body, this is my blood"*

We can now draw the practical conclusions of this doctrine for our daily lives. If at the consecration we too address our brethren with the words, "Take, eat, this is my body; take, drink, this is my blood," we must know what "body" and "blood" mean, so as to know what we are offering.

What did Jesus mean to give us at the Last Supper when he said, "This is my *body*?" In the Bible the word "body" doesn't indicate a component or part of a human being which, united to the other components, the soul and the spirit, forms the complete person. Our way of reasoning is influenced by Greek culture which, in fact, divided man in three parts: body, soul and spirit. In biblical terminology, and therefore in that used by Jesus and Paul, "body" indicates the whole human being in so far as it lives its life in a body, in a corporeal and mortal condition. In his Gospel, John uses the word "flesh" instead of "body" ("if you don't eat the flesh of the Son of man . . . .") and it is obvious that this word in the sixth chapter of the Gospel means the same as in the first chapter where John says "the Word became *flesh*," and that is, human. The word "body" indicates, therefore, the whole of life. In instituting the Eucharist, Jesus left us the gift of his whole life, from the first moment of the incarnation to the very end, including all that had made up his life: silence, sweat, hardship, prayer, struggle, joy, humiliation . . . .

Then Jesus also said: "This is my *blood*." What else does he give us with his blood if he has already given us all his life by giving us his body? He adds death! Having given us his life, he now gives us its most precious part — his death. In the Bible the term "blood" doesn't indicate a part of the body, and therefore a part of a part of a person; it indicates a happening, death. If blood is the seat of life as was thought at that time (cf. Gen 9:4), the shedding of it is the plastic sign of death. "Having loved his own who were in the world, he loved them to the end" (John 13:1). The Eucharist is the mystery of the Body and Blood of the Lord, that is of the life and death of the Lord!

And what do we ourselves offer when we offer our bodies and blood with Jesus at Mass? We offer what Jesus offered: life and death. By "body" we offer all that actually constitutes our physical life: time, health, energy, ability, sentiments, perhaps just a smile, that only a spirit living in a body can give and which is so precious at times. By "blood," we express the offering of our death; not necessarily our final death, or martyrdom for Christ or our brethren. Death means also all that right now prepares and anticipates our death: humiliations, failures, sickness that cripples us, limits due to age or health, everything that "mortifies" us.

22

When St. Paul exhorts us by the mercy of God to present "our bodies," he didn't mean just our senses and carnal appetites, but all of ourselves, body and soul; especially our minds and our wills. In fact he goes on to say: "Do not be conformed to this world but be transformed by the renewal of your mind, that you may prove what is the will of God, what is good and acceptable and perfect" (Rom 12:2).

However, to conform to all this we must start practicing what we have said as soon as we come out from Mass. We must really make the effort, each one within his or her own limits, to offer our "bodies" to our brethren, and that is to say, our time, energy and attention — in a word, our lives. When Jesus had pronounced the words: "Take . . . this is my body; take . . . this is my blood," he didn't allow much time to pass before doing what he had promised: a few hours later he gave his life and blood on the Cross. Otherwise, it's all just empty words, lies. Therefore, after saying to our brothers and sisters: "Take, eat," we must really allow ourselves to be "eaten" and especially by those who do not act with the gentleness and kindness we expect. Jesus said: "What merit have you got if you love only those that love you, greet only those that greet you, invite only those that invite you? Everyone does this" (cf. Matt 5:46-47). On his way to Rome where he was to die a martyr, St. Ignatius of Antioch wrote: "I am the grain of Christ; that I may be ground by the teeth of wild beasts to become pure bread for the Lord."[5] If we think about it, each one of us will realize that there are sharp teeth grinding us: criticisms, contrasts, hidden or open oppositions, different ideas in those surrounding us, differences in character. We should even be grateful to those who help us like this. They are of infinitely more benefit to us than those who approve or flatter us. In another letter, the same holy martyr wrote: "Those that praise me, scourge me."[6]

Let us imagine what would happen if our personal participation in the Mass were to take this form; if at the moment of consecration we were to say, in a loud or low voice, according to each one's role: "Take, eat . . . ." A mother who thus celebrates her Mass, goes home and begins her day made up of a thousand little things. Her life is literally reduced to crumbs but what she does is no little thing: it is Eucharist with Jesus! A religious sister lives her Mass in this way and then goes to her daily work among the old, the sick, children. Her life too might seem split by many

small things that leave no trace at night — another day wasted. But her life too is Eucharist; she has "saved" her own life! A
___ bishop, celebrates his Mass in this way and then
___ nistry, praying, preaching, hearing confessions,
___ iting the sick, listening; his day too is Eucharis-
___ remains one in the breaking of bread, a life spent
___ ole and what makes it whole is the fact that it
___ reat spiritual teacher said: "In the morning, at
___ riest and Jesus is the victim; throughout the day
___ t and I am the victim" (P. Olivaint). So does
___ e "Good Shepherd," because he really gives his
___ .
___ t forget that we have also offered our "blood,"
___ our passiveness, and mortification. It is when
we can no longer do what we want that we can be closer to Christ. After Easter Jesus said to Peter: "When you were young, you girded yourself and walked where you would; but when you are old, you will stretch out your hands, and another will gird you and carry you where you do not wish to go. This he said to show by what death he was to glorify God" (John 21:18ff.). Shortly before this Jesus had said to Peter three times: "Feed my sheep," but now he makes him understand that it is in dying that he will give the greatest glory to God.

Because of the Eucharist there is no such thing as a "useless life" in the world. No one should say: "What use is my life? What am I doing in this world?" You are in the world for the most sublime of reasons, to be a living sacrifice, to be Eucharist with Jesus.

4. *"Come to the Father!"*

The secret lies in a total offering of self, withholding nothing. Jesus was a total oblation on the Cross. There wasn't a cell of his body or sentiment of his heart that he didn't offer to the Father. Anything we withhold for ourselves is lost, because we only possess what we give. St. Francis of Assisi who, because of the elevated fervor of his devotion to the Eucharist can be considered a special guide on the topic, ends his wonderful discourse on the Eucharist with this exhortation: "Look at God's humility, my brothers, and pour out your hearts before him. Humble yourselves that you may be exalted by him. Keep nothing for yourselves, so that he who has given himself wholly to you may receive you wholly.[7] In *The Imitation of Christ,* Jesus says: "Look, I offered myself wholly to the Father for you; I also gave my whole body and blood for you for food, that I might be wholly yours, and you should remain mine. But if you stand upon yourself and do not offer yourself freely to my will, the offering is not fully made, nor will union between us be complete."[8] What we hold back for ourselves to keep a margin of freedom from God pollutes all the rest. It is the little silk thread St. John of the Cross speaks of, which prevents the bird from flying.

Therefore, adopting the sentiments of the author of *The Imitation of Christ* as our own, let us respond to Christ's offering, by giving ourselves totally to him saying: "Lord, all things are yours in heaven and on earth. I long to offer myself to you for a freewill offering, and to remain forever yours. Lord, in the sincerity of my heart, I offer myself to you today to serve forever, for obedience and for a sacrifice of unending praise. Receive me with this holy offering of your precious Body, which today I offer you, in the presence of Angels, invisibly around, that it may be for salvation for me and for all the people."[9]

Yet where can we find the strength to make this total offering of ourselves, to raise ourselves, as it were, with our own hands towards God? The answer is, in the Holy Spirit! Scripture tells us that Christ, through the "eternal Spirit" offered himself to God (Heb 9:14). The Holy Spirit is the source of every act of self-offering. He is the "gift" or better, the very principle of "self-giving": in the Trinity the self-giving of the Father to the Son and of the Son to the Father; in history, the self-giving of God to us and our self-giving to God. It was the Holy Spirit that stirred in the heart of the Word the impulse to offer himself to the Father for us. It is of him then that the liturgy asks in the Mass to "make us an everlasting sacrifice acceptable to God."[10]

Earlier on I mentioned St. Ignatius of Antioch. In his same Letter to the Romans, to convince the local Christians to do nothing to impede his martyrdom, he confides a secret to them: "There is a living spring in me saying: Come to the Father!" It is the unmistakable voice of the Spirit of Jesus which, having returned to the Father, can now say to his disciple: Come, offer yourself with me to the Father!

NOTES

1. St. Augustine, *Sermon* 272 (PL 38. 1247).
2. St. Augustine, *The City of God,* X, 6 (CCL 47, 279).
3. St. Augustine, *Confessions,* X, 43, 69 ("Ideo sacerdos quia sacrificium").
4. St. Gregory of Nazianzus, *Discourses,* 2, 95 (PG 35, 497).
5. St. Ignatius of Antioch, *Letter to the Romans,* 4, 1.
6. St. Ignatius of Antioch, *Letter to the Thrallians,* 4, 1.
7. St. Francis of Assisi, *Letter to a General Chapter,* 2 (*St. Francis of Assisi, Writings and Early Biographies,* Chicago 1983, 106).
8. *The Imitation of Christ,* IV, 8.
9. Ibid.
10. *Eucharistic Prayer* III.

Chapter Three

"He Who Eats Me Will Live Because Of Me"

The Eucharist makes the Church through Communion

An atheist philosopher said: "Man is what he eats," meaning that there is no qualitative difference between matter and spirit in man but that everything in man is reduced to the organic and material component. Once again, without knowing it, an atheist has expressed the Christian mystery in the best way. Because of the Eucharist, a Christian is truly what he eats. Way back, St. Leo the Great wrote: "Our partaking of the Body and Blood of Christ tends only to make us become what we eat."[1]

Let us consider what Jesus says on this point: "As the living Father sent me, and I live because of the Father, so he who eats me will live because of me" (John 6:57). "Because of" refers to two things: the source and the destination. It means that whoever eats the Body of Christ lives "because of" him or due to the life he gives, and he lives "in view of" him, and that is to say, for his glory, his love, his kingdom. As Jesus lives because of and for the Father, so we, by partaking in the sacred mystery of his Body and Blood, live because of and for Jesus.

The Fathers of the Church took the example of physical nourishment to explain this mystery. It is the stronger form of life, they said, that assimilates the weaker and not vice versa. The vegetable world assimilates minerals and animals assimilate vegetables, and the spiritual assimilates the material. To those that receive him, Jesus says: "You shall not change me into your own substance. Instead you shall be changed into me."[2] Food is not a living thing and therefore cannot give us life. It is a source of life only in that it sustains the life we have. Instead the bread of life is a living bread and those who receive it live by it. So, while the food that nourishes the body — fish, bread and every other kind of food — is assimilated by the body and forms human blood, the complete opposite takes place with the bread of life. This bread gives life to those that receive it, assimilates them and transforms them in itself. We are moved by Christ to live the life that is in him, because he is the head and the heart of the whole body. He calls himself the "bread of life" precisely to make us understand that he doesn't nourish us as ordinary food does, but that, as he possesses life, he gives it to us, and he adds: "He who eats me will live because of me."[3] To say that Jesus "assimilates" us in communion signifies, in fact, that he makes us similar to him in our sentiments, desires and our way of thinking; in a word he creates in us "the mind that was in Christ Jesus" (cf. Phil 2:5).

Jesus does this because he is the "heart" of the mystical body. In fact, what is the function of the heart in the human body? The "bad" blood, that is to say, blood impoverished of its vital elements and containing the residue of toxins in the organism, flows back to the heart. In the lungs the blood, reoxygenated and thus regenerated and enriched with nutritive elements, is sent back, by the heart, to all the organs of the body. On a spiritual level, the same thing happens in the heart of the Church, which is Christ. To it flows, at every Mass, the bad blood of the whole world. Into it, at Communion, I throw my sins and blemishes so that they may be destroyed and from it I receive pure blood, his Blood full of life and holiness: the "medicine of immortality," as St. Ignatius of Antioch calls it.[4] It is only when we have experienced this that these words of Scripture can mean something to us: "The blood of Christ . . . will purify your conscience from dead works" (Heb 9:14), and again: "The blood of Jesus cleanses us from all sin" (1 John 1:7). We cannot imagine how truly and really the Eucharist is the "heart" of the Church.

1. *Communion with the Body and Blood of Christ*

Precisely with whom and with what do we enter into communion in the Eucharist? St. Paul says: "The cup of blessing which we bless, is it not a participation in the Blood of Christ? The bread which we break, is it not a participation in the Body of Christ?" (1 Cor 10:6).

We are used to interpreting these words in the sense of participation in the whole person of Christ through what composes it: his body, blood, soul and divinity. This idea depends on Greek anthropology which used to divide human beings into three parts: the body, the soul and the spirit. There is no emphasis on a person-to-person relation, the living to the living, the whole to the entire, which takes place immediately and simultaneously in communion. In biblical language, as I have already said, the words body and blood have a concrete and historical significance; they indicate Christ's whole life or, better still, his life and death. The word body does not so much indicate a metaphysical component of humanity as a state of life, and that is to say, life lived in the body. It indicates the whole person, just like the word "flesh" in John's Gospel. In the Eucharist, the word body designates Christ in his servant state, distinguished by passibility, poverty, the Cross; the Word "made flesh," who worked, sweated, suffered, prayed among us.

The same can be said for the word blood. It does not indicate a part of a part of a human being (blood is part of the body!) but an event: it indicates death. Not any kind of death but a violent one, and in the language of the covenant, an expiatory death (cf. Exod 24:8).

This is an important consequence: there is no moment or experience in Christ's life that we cannot re-live and share in Communion; in fact, his whole life is present and given in his Body and Blood. St. Paul synthesizes the mystery of Christ's Cross, when he says, "he emptied himself" (cf. Phil 2:7). Therefore, one of our Masses could be filled and illuminated with these words, especially if celebrated or assisted at a moment when we have been wronged and feel in a state of total rebellion, or faced with a difficult obedience. Jesus, we can say, emptied himself and I want to empty myself too, by dying to myself and my own "reasons"! This is true "communion" with Christ.

Depending on our disposition or momentary need, we can stay beside Jesus who prays, Jesus who is tempted, Jesus who is tired, Jesus who dies on the Cross and Jesus who rose again, not as a mental pretence but because that same Jesus still exists and is living in the Spirit.

2. *He who is united to the Lord becomes one Spirit with him*

In the well-known mystagogic catechesis attributed to St. Cyril of Jerusalem, we find: "The Body is given to you under the species of bread and the Blood under the species of wine, so that, participating in the Body and Blood of Christ, you may become *concorporeal and consanguineous* with him."[5] Audacious words, but the Fathers knew they were not an exaggeration. The truth is that Eucharistic Communion is so profound that it goes beyond any human comparison we could make. Jesus gives the example of the vine and its branches. This is certainly a very close union; the vine and branches share the same lymph, the same life. When it is separated from the vine, the branch dies. But, being inanimate, neither the vine nor the branches are "aware" of this union! Sometimes the example of spouses is used, who form "one flesh" (it is, perhaps, the strongest comparison); but this is on a different and much more inferior level: that of the flesh and not of the spirit. A married couple may form one flesh, but they cannot form one spirit, if not in a weak moral sense. Instead, "he who is united to the Lord becomes one spirit with him" (1 Cor 6:17). The strength of Eucharistic Communion is precisely that we become one spirit with Jesus and this "one spirit" is ultimately the Holy Spirit!

In the sacrament is repeated each time what came about only once in history; in other words in the Eucharist is repeated what took place in the life of Jesus. It is the Holy Spirit that gave Christ to the world at the moment of his birth (in fact, Mary conceived by the Holy Spirit); at the moment of his death, it is Christ that gave the Holy Spirit to the world (in fact, as he was dying, he "gave up his Spirit" (John 19:30). Likewise in the Eucharist the Holy Spirit gives us Christ in the consecration and Christ gives us the Holy Spirit in the Communion.

It is the Holy Spirit that creates our intimacy with God, St. Basil said.[6] Actually, St. Irenaeus says that the Holy Spirit is "our very communion with Christ."[7] In modern theological language, he is the "immediacy" of our relation with Christ, in the sense that he acts as intermediary between us and him, without setting up any barrier whatever, without placing anything "between" us and Jesus, because, as Jesus and the Father are one, so are Jesus and the Holy Spirit.

In Communion Jesus comes to us as the one who gives the Spirit. Not as the one who gave the Spirit one day, a long time ago, but who, having consumed his bloodless sacrifice on the altar, gives it *now,* he "gives up his Spirit" (cf. John 19:30). Thus he makes us participate in his spiritual unction. His unction is transfused into us; better still, we are immersed in it. "Christ is transfused into us and merges with us, changing us and transforming us in him, like a drop of water poured into an endless sea of fragrant unguent. The effects of this unction on those who receive it are myriad: it does not just limit itself to simply perfuming, and neither to letting them just breathe in its fragrance; it transforms their very substance into the fragrance of the unction which was given up for us: 'We are the aroma of Christ' (2 Cor 2:15)."[8]

Around the Eucharistic table the "sober intoxication of the Spirit" is realized. Commenting on a verse from the Canticle of Canticles, St. Ambrose wrote: " 'I eat my honeycomb with my honey' (Cant 5:1): you see, there is no bitterness in this bread, only sweetness? 'I drink my wine with my milk' (Cant 5:1): you see, this joy is not marred by any blemish? In fact, each time you drink it, your sins are remitted and you become spiritually inebriated. St. Paul warns us: 'Do not get drunk with wine, but be filled with the Spirit' (Eph 5:18); whoever gets drunk with wine staggers and becomes unsteady, but whoever is filled with the Spirit, takes root in Christ, as it were. 'Holy is this inebriation which brings about the sobriety of the heart.' "[9] From this comes the renowned exclamation by the same saint, in a hymn that is still recited today in the Liturgy of the Hours: "Let us joyfully drink the sober abundance of the Spirit!" (*Laeti bibamus sobriam profusionem Spiritus*). Sober inebriation is not just a poetic paradox, it is full of meaning and truth. Drunkenness always transports mortals out of themselves, out of their narrow limits. But, whereas in a normal state of drunkenness (caused by wine, drugs) mortals are transported to live "below" their rational level, almost like beasts, in the state of spiritual inebriation they are transported to live beyond their reason, on God's horizon. Every Communion should end in an ecstasy if by ecstasy we do not mean the extraordinary but accidental phenomena sometimes experienced by the mystics, but simply the "getting out" of oneself (which is what the word literally means), the fact that "it is no longer I that live, but Christ lives in me."

What the Fathers of the Church wanted to say using the symbolic language of inebriation is more rationally expressed by St. Thomas Aquinas when he calls the Eucharist the "sacrament of love" (*sacramentum caritatis*).[10] He explains that love alone brings about union with the living Christ. In fact, love is the only reality through which two separate living beings can become one

31

without losing their individual identity. If the Holy Spirit is said to be "the communion with Christ," it is because he is God's love. A communion that doesn't terminate with an act of love, is incomplete. I communicate wholly and finally with Christ only when I can say, in all simplicity and sincerity of heart, as Peter did: "Lord, you know I love you!" (cf. John 21:16).

3. *"I in them and you in me": communion with the Father*

Through Jesus and his Spirit, in Eucharistic Communion we also reach the Father. In his "priestly prayer" Jesus says to the Father: "That they may be one even as we are one. I in them and thou in me" (John 17:23). The words "I in them and thou in me" signify that Jesus is in us and that the Father is in Jesus. We cannot, therefore, receive the Son without receiving the Father with him. The ultimate reason is that the Father, Son and Holy Spirit have one indivisible divine nature, they are "one." On this point, St. Hilary of Poitiers wrote: "We are united to Christ who is inseparable from the Father, but who, while remaining in the Father, remains united to us. And so, we too reach unity with the Father. In fact, Christ is connaturally in the Father as he was begotten by him; but, in a certain way, we too are connaturally in the Father through Christ. He lives by virtue of the Father and we live by his humanity."[11]

To express ourselves in precise theological terms we should say that in the Eucharist Jesus Christ the Son is *naturally* present (that is, in his divine and human nature) and he is *personally* present (in the person of the Son); *directly,* the Father and the Holy Spirit are only present naturally (by virtue of the unity of the divine nature), whereas *indirectly,* by virtue of the interpenetration (*perichoresis*) of the three divine Persons, they are also present personally. In fact, in each of the three persons of the Trinity, the other two persons are present.

The presence of the whole Trinity in the Eucharist, affirmed by theology, has sometimes been actively experienced by the saints. A great mystic wrote in her diary: "It seemed that in the most Holy Sacrament, as on a throne, I saw the one and triune God: the Father in his omnipotence, the Son in his wisdom, the Holy Spirit in his love. Every time we communicate, our souls and hearts become the temple of the most Holy Trinity, and when

God comes to us, the whole of paradise comes. On seeing God enclosed in the Host, I was transported with joy for the whole day. If I had to give my life to confirm this truth, I would do so a thousand times."[12]

Therefore, we enter into a mysterious communion, real and deep, with the whole Trinity: with the Father, through Christ, in the Holy Spirit. The whole Trinity is invisibly present round the altar. This is depicted in A. Rublëv's well-known icon of the Trinity in which the Father, Son and Holy Spirit, symbolized by the three angels that appeared to Abraham under the oak of Mamre, form a sort of mystic circle round the altar and they seem to say to us: "May you all be one, as we are one!"

4. *God placed his body in our hands*

Communion, therefore, opens, as it were, successive doors to us, by which we first of all enter into Christ's heart and then, through him, into the heart of the Trinity itself. But as soon as we reflect on such kindness on the part of the divinity, sadness invades us. What do we do with the Body of Christ? One day, at the moment of Communion, I was listening to a lovely hymn in which these words were repeated continuously: "God has placed his Body in our hands, God has placed his Body in our hands!" All of a sudden I was seized by a pang of grief: God has placed his Body in our hands but what do we do with God's Body? And I couldn't help crying within myself: We do violence to God! We do violence to him! And we do this by abusing the promise with which he bound himself to come upon the altar and into us. Every day we "oblige" him to make this supreme act of love, but we have no love and are often even distracted, and this is violence. How gentle and kind we must be with a defenseless child; instead, how rough and coarse we are with Jesus who, mysteriously, cannot defend himself from us. St. Francis of Assisi tells us: "Every day Jesus humbles himself just as he did when he came from his heavenly throne into the Virgin's womb; every day he comes to us."[13] Therefore, we cannot receive him if not in a state of deep humility and repentance. Again St. Francis says: "If it is right to honour the Blessed Virgin Mary because she bore him in her holy womb; if St. John the Baptist trembled and was afraid even to touch Christ's sacred head; if the tomb where he lay for only a short time is so venerated; how holy, and virtuous, and worthy should not be the one who receives him into his heart and mouth. . . . Surely this is a great pity, a pitiable weakness, to have him present with you like this and be distracted by anything else in the whole world. Our whole being should be seized with fear, the whole world should tremble and heaven rejoice, when Christ the Son of the living God is present on the altar in the hands of the priest."[14]

Knowing how great is the mystery we receive and how superior to our powers of reception, our friends in heaven — Mary, the angels and the saints — are ready to help us if we ask them. We can talk to them quite simply and resolutely, a little like the man in the Gospels who, having nothing to set before a guest who arrived in the night, did not hesitate to wake up a friend to borrow some loaves from him (cf. Luke 11:5ff.). We can ask these perfect heavenly adorers to lend us their purity, their praise, their humility, their sentiments of infinite gratitude to God and present them to Jesus when we receive him in Communion. The saints, and especially Mary, are ready to do this. They can do it because of the communion of saints; they wish to do so because they love us and Jesus. Of course, they will not refuse us! Actually, I think there is a certain competition and jealousy in heaven for such requests. In Communion God is involved and when God is involved the impossible can happen: simple wishes, no matter how childish, are considered as rights by divine omnipotence and generosity. "He who did not spare his own Son but gave him up for us all, will he not also give us all things with him" (Rom 8:32). If a king allows his son to visit a poor wretch in his hovel, will he refuse the poor fellow a few things to make the hovel less squalid and unworthy of the visit? We can become even more like children and at the moment of Communion picture Jesus's "surprise" when we receive him and he expects to find the usual squalid place, whereas, instead, he finds himself surrounded by the same heavenly splendour he has come from!

But we must be on the alert. Mary and the saints take what concerns the King of Heaven very seriously and how sad and embarrassing it would be if, halfway through the day, we were suddenly to realize they had come and adorned the house, but the owner had gone out early and not returned!

I think it is a salutary grace for a Christian to go through a

34

period when he or she fears to receive Holy Communion, trembles at the thought of what is about to happen and repeats over and over again like John the Baptist: "Do you come to me?" (Matt 3:14). We can only receive God as "God," safeguarding, that is, his holiness and majesty. We cannot domesticate God! Church preaching should not fear — now that Communion has become so common and "easy" — to repeat to the faithful, sometimes, what the Letter to the Hebrews says: "You have not come to what may be touched, a blazing fire and darkness, and gloom, and a tempest, and the sound of a trumpet, and a voice whose words made the hearers entreat that no further messages be spoken to them. . . . Indeed, so terrifying was the sight that Moses said, 'I tremble with fear.' But you have come to Mount Zion and to the city of the living God, the heavenly Jerusalem, and to innumerable angels in festive gathering, and to the assembly of the first-born who are enrolled in heaven, and to a judge who is God of all . . . and to the Mediator of a new covenant, and to the sprinkled blood that speaks more graciously than the blood of Abel" (Heb 12:18-24).

We know the warning that re-echoed in liturgical assemblies at the beginning of the Church, at the moment of Communion: "Let whoever is holy approach, let whoever is not holy repent!"[15] St. John Chrysostom, who had to deal with people inclined to take things lightly, never spoke of Eucharistic Communion without using the adjective "terrible" (*friktos*): "Terrible," he wrote, "are the mysteries of the Church; terrible is the altar!" "Terrible and ineffable is the communion of the holy mysteries"; "Without the special help of God's grace, no human soul could bear the fire of this sacrifice without being completely destroyed."[16] The same saint used to say that after Communion, a Christian is like a lion emitting flames from his mouth: the devil cannot bear his sight.[17] We need to experience, at least once, the terrible majesty of the Eucharist to be able to fully appreciate God's goodness and condescension which keeps veiled from us this majesty so as not to destroy us.

5. *Communion with the body of Christ, the Church*

So far we have limited ourselves to communion seen vertically, communion with God the Father, the Son and the Holy Spirit. But there is also a horizontal communion and that is with our brothers and sisters. In the text mentioned at the beginning, St. Paul said: "The bread which we break, is it not a participation in the Body of Christ? Because there is one bread, we who are many are one body, for we all partake of the one bread" (1 Cor 10:16-17). The word "body" recurs twice; the first time it designates the real Body of Christ and the second time his mystical body, the Church. We could not express more simply and clearly that Eucharistic Communion is at the same time both communion with God and communion among us.

St. Augustine wrote: "Having suffered the passion, the Lord gave us his Body and Blood in the sacrament, so that we should become these things. In fact we are his body and through his mercy we are what we receive. Just think what the element of bread was when it was still in the field: the earth germinated the seed and rain nourished it; then it was taken to the threshing floor, sifted and placed in the granary. Later it was ground and baked and bread was made of it. Think now of yourselves: you didn't exist and you were created; you were placed on the Lord's threshing floor and threshed by the "oxen," that is by those who told you the good news. As catechumens you were stored in the granary; when you were given your names at baptism, you began to be 'ground' by fastings and exorcisms; then, finally, you came to the water, you were kneeded and you became one. The fire of the Holy Spirit came upon you and you were baked and became the bread of the Lord. This is what you received. As you see, the bread is one, so you too are one, loving one another, keeping the same faith, the same hope and undivided charity."[18]

The body of Christ, the Church, was formed in the image of the Eucharistic bread: it went through the same vicissitudes. The Eucharistic bread achieves the unity of the members signifying it (*significando causat*). In Communion "the unity of God's people is suitably signified and wondrously brought about."[19] In other words, what the bread and wine visibly symbolize — through the unity of many grains of wheat and the multiplicity of grapes — the sacrament achieves on an interior and spiritual level.

"It achieves it": not, however, automatically on its own but together with our commitment. I can no longer disinterest myself in brothers or sisters when I receive the Eucharist; I cannot reject them without rejecting Christ himself and cutting myself off from the unity. Those who pretend to be full of fervor for Christ at Communion, when they have just offended or hurt a brother or sister without saying they are sorry, or intending to do so, are like those who, meeting a friend after a long time bend forward to affectionately kiss him but don't realize that, in the meantime, they are trampling on his feet with nailed boots! Christ's feet are the members of his body, especially the poorest and most humiliated. He loves those "feet" and could rightly cry out: You honor me in vain!

The Christ I receive in Communion is the same undivided Christ the person next to me receives. He unites us one to the other while uniting us all to himself. Herein, perhaps, lies the deep significance of what is written in the New Testament and in the early writings of the Church. The early Christians felt united "in the breaking of bread" (Acts 2:42). A paradox — united in dividing. In fact, breaking means dividing. It is just like that: we are united in dividing, or better, in sharing, the same bread! St. Augustine reminded us earlier on that there can be no bread if the grains of wheat haven't first been "ground." There is nothing better than fraternal charity to grind us, especially if we are members of a community: bearing with one another, in spite of all the differences in character, outlook, etc. It is like a millstone that, day by day, refines our roughness.

Now we have seen what it means to say *Amen* and to whom we say *Amen* at the moment of Communion. The priest proclaims: "The Body of Christ!" and we answer: *Amen!* We say *Amen* to the most sacred Body of Jesus born of the Virgin Mary and who died and rose again for us. But we also say *Amen* to his mystical body, the Church, and precisely to those close to us in life or at the Eucharistic table. We cannot separate the two bodies and accept one without the other. To many of our brothers and sisters, perhaps to most of them, it will be no effort on our part to say *Amen,* yes, I welcome you! But there will always be among them someone that causes us suffering, whoever is to blame; someone who opposes us or criticizes or speaks badly of us. In this case it is more difficult to say *Amen,* but it hides a special grace. There is, actually, a sort of secret in this little act. When

37

we want a more intimate communion with Jesus or we need forgiveness or a special grace from him, this is the way to obtain
it: to welcome Jesus in Communion together with that particular
brother or sister. We can say, clearly, to Jesus: "Jesus, I receive
you today together with . . . (better if we here name the person);
I'll keep him or her in my heart with you; I shall be happy if you
bring him or her with you." This little act is very pleasing to Jesus
because he knows that it causes us to die a little.

I shall conclude this chapter with a verse from the *Adoro Te
Devote* that has nourished the Eucharistic devotion of so many
generations of believers:

> "O Thou, memorial of our Lord's own dying.
> O living bread, to mortals life supplying!
> Make Thou my soul henceforth on Thee to live;
> Ever a taste of heavenly sweetness give."

NOTES

1. St. Leo the Great, *Sermon 12 on the Passion,* 7 (CCL 138A, 338).
2. St. Augustine, *Confessions,* VII, 10.
3. Cf. N. Cabasilas, *Life in Christ,* IV, 3 (PG 150, 597).
4. St. Ignatius of Antioch, *Letter to the Ephesians,* 20, 2.
5. St. Cyril of Jerusalem, *Mystagogical Catecheses,* IV, 3 (PG 33, 1100).
6. St. Basil the Great, *On the Holy Spirit,* XIX, 49 (PG 32, 157).
7. St. Irenaeus, *Against Heresies,* III, 24, 1.
8. N. Cabasilas, *Life in Christ,* IV, 3 (PG 150, 593).
9. St. Ambrose, *On the Sacraments,* V, 17 (PL 16, 449f.).
10. St. Thomas Aquinas, *Theological Summa,* I-IIae, q. 28, a. 1; III,
    q. 78, a. 3.
11. St. Hilary of Poitiers, *On the Trinity,* VIII, 13–16 (PL 10, 246f.).
12. St. Veronica Giuliani, *Diary,* entry 30 May, 1715 (ed. Città di Castello
    1973, vol. III, 928).
13. St. Francis of Assisi, *Admonitions,* I (*Writings,* 78).
14. St. Francis of Assisi, *Letter to a General Chapter* (*Writings,* 105).
15. *Didache,* X, 6.
16. St. John Chrysostom, *Homilies on the Gospel of John,* 46, 4 (PG
    59, 261); *On the Priesthood,* 3, 4 (PG 48, 642).
17. St. John Chrysostom, *Baptismal Catecheses,* III, 12 (SCh 50, 158).
18. St. Augustine, *Sermon Denis* 6 (PL 46, 834f.).
19. Vatican II, *Lumen gentium,* 11.

Chapter Four

"Unless You Drink the Blood of the Son of Man . . ."

The Eucharist, Communion with the Blood of Christ

This chapter is a continuation of our reflection on "The Eucharist makes the Church through Communion." So far we have discussed communion in general, so we shall now center our attention on the particular aspect of communion with the Blood of Christ.

One day, at the end of Mass, a woman handed me a note which said, "Jesus tells us, 'Take and drink all of you, this is my Blood.' Why can't we then drink the Blood of Christ as he told us? His Blood is sufficiently powerful to wash away our sins and we thirst for it. Why should we be deprived of this? There are grapes and wine in abundance in our fields to supply all lay Christians with the Blood of Christ everyday if they want it. Why are we so ungenerous with him when he is so generous with us?" Talking to her a little later, I realized that her question did not spring from a spirit of contradiction but from a real longing for the Blood of Christ. This teaching is an answer to this longing that is becoming more and more widespread among Christians. The aim is to help us rediscover the power and sweetness of the Eucharistic Blood of Christ and to encourage the practice of communion under both kinds now that Vatican Council II has restored it in the Catholic Church.

1. *Communion under both kinds*

By way of introduction I wish to make a few historical and theological remarks which, I think, all can understand. Jesus instituted the Eucharist under the signs of bread and wine, that is, under the signs of eating and drinking which, together, complete the image of the banquet and supper. In his teaching at Capernaum he said, "Unless you eat the flesh of the Son of man and drink his blood, you have no life in you." And again he said, "My flesh is food indeed, and my blood is drink indeed" (John 6:53, 55). When he instituted the Eucharist he said, "Take and eat, take and drink all of you." He did not say "some of you" or "whichever of you wants" but "all of you."

St. Paul testifies how this command was faithfully carried out in the apostolic Church when he once mentions "communion in the blood of Christ" even before mentioning "communion in the body of Christ" (1 Cor 10:16).

It is sufficient to recall what the Blood of Christ represented in the Eucharistic teachings of the Fathers of the Church by mentioning just a few of them. St. Augustine used to say to the neophytes, "See in the Bread the body that hung from the cross and in the chalice the Blood that came out from his side. . . . Eat this bond of your unity so as not to be scattered; drink this price paid for you so as not to be debased."[1] "The blood of Christ is the price of our redemption" (1 Cor 6:20; Eph 1:7). The faithful are "precious" because of the "price" *(pretium)* Christ paid for them. "If," exclaimed St. John Chrysostom, "you show the evil one your tongue moistened with the precious Blood, he will not be able to resist it; if you show him your mouth tinged with red, he will shun you like a frightened beast. Do you want to know the power of this Blood? Then just see where it came from and where its source was—the cross and the Lord's side."[2]

The love and reverence of the early Christians for the Blood of Christ is clear from how they received it. "When you have received the Body of Christ," a bishop told his congregation, "then receive the chalice of his Blood. Do not stretch out your hands but bowing low say Amen in adoration and veneration, and sanctify yourselves by receiving the Blood of Christ. Dry your lips with your fingers and then touch your forehead, your eyes and your senses to sanctify them. And raise thanks to God who judged you worthy to participate in this mystery."[3]

This love and reverence for the Eucharist gave origin to one of the most beloved symbols of the Eucharist, the pelican. In ancient times it was commonly believed that the pelican pierced its breast with its beak to nourish its hungry offspring with its own blood.

If, from all these premises, we observe how the Eucharist was observed for a long time, we cannot but notice how far we have

moved away from its original character. Various factors have in-
advertently led to the Eucharist becoming much more the sacrament of the Body of Christ and much less of his Blood. The first
of these is communion only under the sign of bread. Eucharistic
worship, outside the Mass, made its unintentional contribution
too. Only the host is used for exposition, adoration, and benedic-
tion of the Eucharist, and on the feast of Corpus Christi only the
Body of Christ is carried in procession. Some of the most traditional of the Eucharistic hymns ("Ave Verum," "Panis Angeli-
cus") suggestively but unilaterally present the Eucharist as "the
true Body born of Mary," and the "bread of Angels," without
even a mention of his Blood. The Blood of Christ seems to be
the "poor relative," an appendix of the Body of Christ, with the
result that the Eucharist seems to signify more the mystery of the
incarnation rather than the passion.

Christian worship tried to remedy this drawback by develop-
ing, outside the Eucharistic mystery, a flourishing devotion to the
Blood of Christ. The institution of a separate feast for the Precious Blood, on July 1, is proof of this: as if the feast of the Body
of Christ was not the feast of his Blood too. This feast was abol-
ished after Vatican Council II while, in parallel, the feast of the
"Most Holy Body of Christ" was again given its original name
of the "Feast of the Most Holy Body and Blood of Christ."

However, let us return to the main point of communion under
the two kinds. We know that this was the normal practice in the
Roman Church toward the end of the twelfth century. In the fifth
century, Pope Gelasius even went as far as condemning those who
did not communicate also with the Blood of Christ, saying, "They
should receive the whole sacrament or be deprived of it altogether.
It is, in fact, sacrilegious to divide this mystery which is one and
identical."[4] Later on, for practical reasons ("Christians have in-
creased in number and include the aged, the young and children
who are not always able to ensure the proper devotion due to the
sacrament"), this practice was gradually abandoned and communion with the chalice was reserved only for the celebrant.

It is useful to know the theological reasons given for this liturgical practice. It is based on the certainty that "Jesus Christ is
present whole and entire in each of the two kinds." On citing this
principle, St. Thomas Aquinas immediately explains its meaning
and limits. "It is true," he says, "that Christ whole and entire
is present in each of the two kinds but for different reasons."

In fact, under the sign of bread the Body of Christ is present "in virtue of the sacrament," that is in virtue of the word of Christ, whereas the Blood is only present "in virtue of natural concomitance," that is in virtue of the fact that wherever there is a living body there is necessarily its blood too. Likewise the Blood of Christ is present under the sign of wine "in virtue of the sacrament," whereas the Body of Christ is present only indirectly on the principle of "natural concomitance."[5]

The drawback arises when the principle of "natural concomitance" prevails over Christ's will expressed in the words he used at the institution, that is, over the "sacrament" (i.e., when the philosophical idea of the moment prevails over biblical thought and determines the liturgical practice). We have several times recalled that for Aristotle, and indeed for us too, the word *blood* usually just signifies a part of the human body. This would necessarily lead us to conclude that in virtue of the natural concomitance Blood is not the only thing present in the Body of Christ but that there are also nerves and bones, the heart, the hands, and so on. But all this emphasizes the crude material aspect and averts our attention from the true meaning of the rite instituted by Christ. In the Bible and in the words of institution, blood is far from being just a simple part of the human body! It is significant that the only arguments that could be advanced in the place of Scripture and tradition for the new liturgical practice were an "ordinary Gloss" and the "use of many churches."[6]

St. Thomas himself reveals a certain reserve in applying the principle of "real concomitance," especially in the objections he raises against his thesis. "This sacrament," he wrote, "is celebrated in memory of the Lord's passion, but the Lord's passion is better expressed by his Blood than by his Body and so we should abstain from receiving his Body rather than his Blood."[7] On the other hand, if we strictly apply the principle that the Body already contains the Blood, we get the idea that one of the two kinds is superflous and that Christ need not have included it. The saint explains, "Neither of the two kinds is superflous. First of all because they serve to give a true representation of Christ's passion during which his Blood was separated from his Body. In the second place, the fact of offering the faithful the Body of Christ to eat and his Blood to drink separately, conforms with the nature of this sacrament."[8]

However, we can see that in this phase and in spite of every-

42

thing the Church still saw the importance of communion with the Blood of Christ. As in many other cases, communion with Christ's Blood was finally abandoned in both theory and practice, as a reaction to the positions taken by the Protestant Reformers. The Council of Trent did not condemn the practice of communion under both kinds but it did condemn the theological reasons advanced for it which claimed that Christ was not present all and entire in each kind.[9] In fact, the council left the question open to possible practical concessions. It was only in 1621 that the practice of communion under both kinds was finally suppressed. This was yet another sad consequence of the division among Christians. What was compromised in this new practice was obviously not the essence and validity of the sacrament but the perfection and completion of the sign. Both the bread and the wine were still consecrated and at least at every Mass the celebrant communicated also with the Blood of Christ.

Today, Vatican Council II has again made communion under both kinds possible. It stated that, "The dogmatic principles laid down by the Council of Trent [that Christ, whole and entire is present in each of the two kinds] remaining intact, communion under both kinds may be granted when the bishops think fit, not only to clerics and religious, but also to the laity, in cases to be determined by the Apostolic See."[10] Communion under both kinds is not only allowed but encouraged. An official text states, "Holy Communion more completely expresses its nature of sign when it is received under both kinds. The sign of the Eucharistic banquet is more evident and the divine will to sanction the new and everlasting covenant in the Lord's Blood is more clearly expressed, and the link between the Eucharistic banquet and the eschatological banquet of the Father's kingdom is clearer."[11]

The new missal lists fourteen cases when the faithful may be given the chalice at communion. Episcopal conferences added other occasions and we may hope that the day will soon come when all those who so wish may receive Christ's Blood at communion. Indeed, how long can a practice last that discriminates between Mass and Mass and between one person and another within the same Mass, without the communion under both kinds itself becoming a sign of distinction and not of communion among the faithful? It must be admitted that the norms fixed by the ecclesiastical authorities on this point were not enforced to the full; in fact much more could be done.

However, it would be of little value to restore communion under both kinds, even on a general level, without the support of a specific catechesis explaining the significance of Christ's Blood and creating desire for it. Otherwise, the sign *(sacramentum)* would be restored as it were, but not its significance or reality *(res sacramenti)*. This is the aim of the following reflection. Let the cry of St. Ignatius, the martyr, burst from our hearts: "I long for the bread of God which is the flesh of Jesus Christ, and for his Blood to drink which is incorruptible love!"[12] We must separate the "Most Precious Blood" from the sphere of "devotion" where it has so often been confined and restore it to its proper place in kerygma and sacrament, so that it may again mean what it meant to Paul and the other apostles who condensed the whole of redemption and all God's love for humanity in the word *blood*.

2. *Blood in the Bible: figure, event, and sacrament*

The theme of blood is like a sort of scarlet thread or a small stream of fire that goes throughout the Bible from beginning to end and reaches us in the Eucharist. In trying to follow this thread it is of help to us to look at the scheme illustrated at the beginning of the book according to which the Eucharist is present in the whole history of salvation, respectively as a *figure* in the Old Testament, as an *event* in the life of Jesus and as a *sacrament* in the Church. In the light of this scheme we see the shedding of Christ's Blood first of all *prophetically* prefigured, then *historically* fulfilled and finally *sacramentally* renewed in the Eucharist.

The main figures of Christ's Blood in the Old Testament are the Passover lamb (Exod 12:7-13), the blood of the covenant that Moses threw upon the people (cf. Exod 24:8), and the blood for the atonement of sins with which the high priest entered the holy place on the day of the great atonement (cf. Lev 16:1ff.). All these figures did not lose their importance when Christ really shed his blood on the cross. Actually, they serve to describe and interpret it and highlight its absolute superiority over all the prefigurations.

In the words he used at the institution, Jesus himself recalls these three figures with words like "memorial" (cf. Exod 12:14), the "blood of the new covenant" and "for the forgiveness of sins." The apostolic teaching follows this line. In his first letter

Peter writes, "You know that you were ransomed from the futile ways inherited from your fathers, not with perishable things such as silver and gold, but with the precious blood of Christ like that of a lamb without blemish or spot" (1 Pet 1:18-19). This concerned the Passover lamb. Then in the Letter to the Hebrews, to counterpoint the ancient rites, a whole chapter talks of Christ's blood as being the principle of the new and everlasting covenant and the atonement of sins: "Christ entered once for all into the Holy Place, taking not the blood of goats and calves, but his own blood, thus securing an eternal redemption" (Heb 9:12).

The figures of the Old Testament are the background to the development of the splendid teachings of the Fathers of the Church. In a comment on Exodus 12:13 ("When I see the blood, I will protect you"), one of them wrote, "Jesus, you have truly protected us from being destroyed. Like a father you stretched out your arms and hid us in the shadow of your wings when you shed your divine Blood on the earth as a libation for the love of mankind."[13]

As I have said, these figures and realities come to us in the Eucharist like a small stream of fire. But there is an important novelty which is characteristic of the sacrament. In the place of blood we have its sign, wine. There is an affinity between wine and blood; wine is the "blood of the grape" (Deut 32:14). "It avoids the natural horror that blood provokes while keeping intact the efficacy of the price of Redemption."[14] And not only this but the blood-wine transposition gives these words of Jesus a precise meaning, "My blood is drink indeed"; it evokes the "new wine," that of the true vine, suggested by the wine at the wedding of Cana; it recalls the theme of spiritual joy and gladness of heart (Ps 104:15) thus making the Eucharist a foretaste of the heavenly banquet of the kingdom of God and the marriage supper of the Lamb (cf. Mark 14:25; Rev 19:9).

"The Holy Spirit," wrote St. Cyprian, "is not silent about the mystery of this Blood." In fact, in the psalms he tells us, "My cup overflows" (cf. Ps 23:6). The gladness of heart that comes from the Lord's chalice and his Blood is not, however, the same as that from ordinary wine. The Lord's chalice gladdens the heart of man to make him sober and it leads souls to spiritual wisdom. And if ordinary wine distends the mind and relaxes the spirit, dispersing all unhappiness, the Lord's Blood and the chalice of salvation dispel the memory of the old self making us forget old habits and freeing us from all unhappiness accumulated in our hearts for our sins, for the joy of divine forgiveness."[15] It is with all this in mind that we still exclaim today, in a well-known prayer, "Blood of Christ, inebriate me!"

Mystagogical teaching needs poetry for its full expression since it is itself a sublime type of poetry that "sings," more than "investigates," the mysteries of faith. Let us now listen to a great Catholic poet as he sings his praises of the "Precious Blood" in its Eucharistic form and may we be infected with his enthusiasm:

> This Blood given him by Mary
> And the warmth of his own heart,
> This Blood he shared with her,
> Is now given to us in the glorious sleep
> Of the sacramental inebriation! . . .
> It is not only a gold chalice
> That we raise in our hands,
> It is the whole sacrifice of Calvary! . . .
> The whole of Redemption is before us,
> Like a leaning vase,
> Like the five rivers of Paradise . . .
> Our lips rest on the life to come.[16]

From the five wounds of Christ on the cross flow the rivers that water the new Paradise, which is the Church (cf. Gen 2:10). Thanks to the Eucharist we become "kinsmen" of Christ[17] and, more remotely, of Mary too. What is said of the Body of Jesus in the "Ave Verum" could also be said of his Blood, "Hail to Thee! true Blood, sprung from the Virgin Mary's womb. . . ."

At this point we might wonder why so much importance is given to such a material thing as blood, which in some ways we even find disgusting because of the images of suffering and violence it evokes. What is there about blood to justify its importance in biblical worship? The answer is that in the Bible blood, including Christ's, is of no importance in itself as such. For ancient man blood was the seat of life. Therefore, the spilling of blood was (when, as for Jesus, it was one's own blood and not someone else's or an animal's) a sign of a love of which there is no greater love (cf. John 15:13). "It was not the Son's death that pleased the Father, so much as his will to die spontaneously for us."[18] The blood is the sign of obedience to the Father and love for us, even to death. Christ "loves us and has freed us from our sins by his blood" (Rev 1:5). Christ's Eucharistic Blood was called "the tremendous chalice of love"[19] thus presenting the Eucharist to us in very few words as the mystery of loving condescension and, at the same time, of absolute transcendence, as a "tremendous and fascinating mystery," like God himself.

St. Catherine of Siena, who had great love for the Blood of Christ, wrote to her confessor: "Drown yourself in the Blood of Christ crucified, bathe yourself in the Blood, inebriate and satiate yourself with the Blood and clothe yourself in the Blood. And if you are unfaithful, baptize yourself again in the Blood; if the devil has blurred your mind's eye, cleanse your eyes with the Blood; if you become ungrateful for unseen gifts, be grateful in the Blood. . . . Melt your lukewarmness in the heat of the Blood and in the light of the Blood darkness will dissolve and you will be the spouse of Truth."[20] At a first reading of these impassioned words the gentle Catherine might appear bloodthirsty; but if we substitute the "love of Christ" for the "Blood of Christ" all will be clear.

However, we must beware of reducing the Blood of Christ to a pure symbol, even if that symbol be the great reality of love. A "symbol" is something that suggests or recalls something else, a material reality standing for a spiritual reality. But Christ's Blood is not just the symbol of a spiritual reality—his love and obedience—it stands for a precise event in time and space: "Christ entered once for all into the Holy Place, taking his own blood, thus securing an eternal redemption" (Heb 9:12). It is this that gives it its unique and transcendent power. It is both a sign and a memorial. It does not just create a vertical relationship between a visible and an invisible reality but also a historical, horizontal relationship between the present sign and the past event. It places us in direct contact, even if only sacramental, with the death of Christ. Christ's blood is like a glowing seal on the Bible attesting that "everything has been fulfilled."

3. *"All were made to drink of one Spirit"*

St. Paul says that God put forward Jesus Christ as an expiation "by his blood to be received by faith" (Rom 3:25). It seems then, that it is faith and not the sacrament that puts us in contact

47

with the mysterious power of Christ's blood. The truth is that both are necessary and must be kept united. Faith is certainly the means but its full and practical expression is in the sacrament of the Eucharist. It is in the Eucharist that the free gift of justification through faith is renewed. The blood of the new covenant is consecrated and lifted up before you just as the serpent was lifted up in the desert (cf. John 3:14). You believe that this is the same blood as was shed for you on the cross; you recall the words: "The blood of Jesus cleanses us from all sin" (1 John 1:7). Therefore, cast all your sins into it like stones into a lime furnace to be crushed and, like the tax collector, return home each time "justified" (Luke 18:14) and that is, forgiven and made new.

Occasionally, when I raise the chalice after the consecration, I like to linger over it. If I know of situations where struggle and sin are particularly hard, I mentally proclaim the power of the Blood of Christ over them, sure that there is nothing more efficacious to oppose the threatening power of darkness and evil. "If by just seeing the sight of blood on the Hebrews doorposts, the angel of death was afraid to enter their houses to slay them (cf. Exod 12:23), how much quicker will the devil flee when faced with the reality?"[21]

Communion with the Body of Christ can already give us all this grace if accompanied by lively faith in the Blood of Christ. Yet, communion with the chalice is the best way to accede to this because "it causes what it signifies," as do all sacramental signs. The Letter to the Hebrews says that "the blood of Christ . . . purifies our conscience from dead works" (Heb 9:14). Our sins sink to the bottom of our consciences like dead weights. What a relief it is to discover that the Eucharist can always free us from these dead weights that crush us. "If each time the Blood is shed, it is shed for the remission of sins, then I must always receive it for it always remits my sins; I sin always so I must always avail myself of the medicine."[22]

However, Christ's Blood doesn't have only this so to say negative effect; there is also the extremely positive effect of giving us the Holy Spirit. An ancient author wrote: "Through the Blood shed for us, we receive the Holy Spirit. The Blood and the Spirit have been linked so that by the Blood, which is part of our nature, we should be able to receive the Holy Spirit, which is beyond our nature."[23] Blood, like its sign wine, is somewhat similar to fire in color and heat ("fluid fire," as they are sometimes called!) and fire, in its turn, recalls the Holy Spirit. As one of the oldest Passover homilies puts it, "We drink the chalice of joy, the living and burning Blood, signed with the heat of the Spirit."[24] Using the words of Jesus, St. Ephrem says, "I give you wine to drink in which fire and Spirit are mingled."[25]

The expression of this idea was influenced by the belief of the time that blood was the seat and channel, as it were, of the *pneuma* in the human body, but in content this idea comes from the Bible. John saw a close relationship between the Spirit Jesus "gave up" on the cross and the blood and water that immediately after came from his side (cf. John 19:30-34), so much so that in his First Letter he says, "There are three witnesses, the Spirit, the water and the blood" (1 John 5:8). When St. Paul wrote, "All were made to drink of one Spirit" (1 Cor 12:13), he was establishing the same link between the Eucharistic drink and the Holy Spirit. And when commenting on the water that came out of the rock (cf. Exod 17:5f.) he said, "They drank from a spiritual rock and the rock was Christ" (1 Cor 10:4). So the Christian people also have their "spiritual rock," from which they receive a "spiritual drink," the Holy Spirit. And thanks to the Eucharist this rock has "accompanied" them throughout history and will continue to do so. "For them water came from the rock, for you there is the Blood; the water quenched their thirst for a time, the Blood washes you forever."[26] For this reason communion with the Blood of Christ is the surest way to receive the Holy Spirit.

In conclusion, what can we do to restore the Blood of Christ to its rightful place in theology and Christian devotion? Besides rediscovering its importance in the Bible and spreading the practice of communion under both kinds, little practical things could be done, with the local bishop's permission, to help the faithful to an awareness of the Eucharist as the sacrament of both the Body and Blood of Christ. For example, a transparent chalice of glass or crystal could occasionally be used at Mass to allow the people to see for themselves Christ's Blood as they see his Body in the host. In particular circumstances Eucharistic adoration could be done before the Body and Blood of Christ, or even just before the Blood to remind people that the whole Christ is present in the Blood too; then, on the feast of Corpus Christi, the Lord's Blood could be carried in procession together with his Body. Obviously wine is not as easily preserved as bread but it would be necessary to keep it only for the occasion.

I have mentioned that the "Precious Blood" must be removed from the sphere of devotion and clearly placed in the sphere of kerygma and sacrament. And this would not be a rejection of all the valid and splendid things the Church has received from this devotion over the last centuries. On the contrary, it would give all this a sound dogmatic basis. Faith does not exclude devotion. It kindles it, especially when it is addressed directly to God or to Christ. Even the countless religious institutes founded in the last centuries and bearing the name of the Precious Blood could find this a help to discover the beauty of their particular charism and to live it in a way ever more consonant with the renewed biblical and liturgical feeling of our days.

Let us conclude with the words used by generations of believers before us to express their ardent longing for the Blood of Christ:

> O Loving Pelican! O Jesus, Lord!
> Unclean I am, but cleanse me in Thy Blood,
> Of which a single drop, for sinners spilt,
> Can purge the entire world from all its guilt.

Each time we return to our places after receiving the Eucharist, especially if we have also received it under the sign of wine, these fascinating and yet admonitory words of Scripture should resound in our inner hearts: "You have come . . . to Jesus the mediator of a new covenant and to the sprinkled blood that speaks more graciously than the blood of Abel" (Heb 12:24).

NOTES

1. St. Augustine, *Sermon Denis* 3, 3 (Misc.Agost. 1, 19).
2. St. John Chrysostom, *Baptismal Catecheses* 3, 12.16 (SCh 50, 158f.).
3. St. Cyril of Jerusalem, *Mystagogical Catecheses* V, 22 (PG 33, 1125).
4. Pope Gelasius, *Canons* (PL 59, 14).
5. St. Thomas Aquinas, *Theologica Summa* III, q. 76, a. 2.
6. Ibid., III, q. 76, a. 2; q. 80, a. 12, *sed contra*.
7. Ibid., III, q. 80, a. 12.
8. Ibid., III, q. 76, a. 2.
9. Denzinger-Schönmetzer, *Enchiridion Symbolorum,* nr. 1725–1734.
10. Vatican II, *Sacrosanctum Concilium,* 55.
11. Instruction on the Worship of the Eucharistic Mystery, *Eucharisticum Mysterium* 32 (AAS 59, 1967) 558.
12. St. Ignatius of Antioch, *Letter to the Romans* 7, 3.
13. *Ancient Paschal Homily* 38 (SCh 27, 159).

14. St. Ambrose, *On the Sacraments,* IV, 20.
15. St. Cyprian, *Epist.* 63, 11 (PL 4, 394).
16. P. Claudel, *The Precious Blood* (*Oeuvre Poétique,* Paris, Gallimard 1967) 541f.
17. St. Cyril of Jerusalem, *Mystagogical Catecheses* IV, 3 (PG 33, 1100).
18. St. Bernard, *On the Error of Abelard* 8, 21 (PL 182, 1070).
19. N. Cabasilas, *Life in Christ* III, 3 (PG 150, 580).
20. St. Catherine of Siena, *Letter* 102.
21. St. John Chrysostom, *Baptismal Catecheses* III, 15 (SCh 50, 160).
22. St. Ambrose, *On the Sacraments* IV, 28.
23. *Paschal Homilies in the tradition of Origen II,* 7 (SCh 36, 83).
24. *Ancient Paschal Homily* 8 (SCh 27, 133f.).
25. St. Ephrem Syrus, *Sermon for the Holy Week* 2, 627 (CSCO 413, 41).
26. St. Ambrose, *On the Mysteries* 8, 48.

Chapter Five

"Do This In Memory Of Me"

The Eucharist makes the Church through Contemplation

So far I have tried to demonstrate how the Eucharist makes the Church through consecration and through communion. I now want to add that there is another way in which the Eucharist makes the Church and that is, contemplation.

The Eucharist and contemplation have been seen, at times, as two distinct, almost parallel ways to Christian perfection. The first way is objective, or *mysteric,* and gives prime importance to the sacraments (mysteries) and especially to the Eucharist; the second way is subjective, or *mystic,* and gives primacy to contemplation. There is a certain diversification between the patristic epoch and the modern epoch, and between Eastern and Western spirituality. Patristic spirituality, to which Eastern spirituality sticks more closely, is said to be based more on the mysteries; Western spirituality, instead, influenced by some of the great modern mystics, is more based on contemplation.

Whatever the case really is (it is always more complex than the schemata), I think it is time to make a synthesis of these two ways, or better still, to rediscover the synthesis that existed on this point for centuries and which, for various reasons, has been lost. According to this unitarian point of view, sacraments and prayer are not two different and alternative "ways" to sanctification, for they are closely bound and interdependent. The sacramental life is certainly at the base of everything, the "mysteries" put us into immediate and objective contact with the redemption worked by God in Christ Jesus, once and for all. Yet, they alone are not sufficient to make us advance in the spiritual life. An inner life of contemplation must support the sacramental life. In fact, contemplation is the means through which we "receive," in a strong sense, the mysteries, and through which we interiorize them and open ourselves to their action. It is the existential and subjective side of the mysteries; it allows the grace received in the sacraments

53

to mold our inner being, that is, our thoughts, feelings, will and memory.

Only when the divine life we receive in the sacraments has been assimilated in contemplation, can it be practically expressed in action — in the practice of the virtues and especially charity. Just as there is no human action that doesn't originate in thought (if it does, it is useless, or extremely dangerous), there is no Christian virtue that doesn't originate in contemplation. St. Gregory of Nyssa wrote: "There are three facts that manifest a Christian's life and distinguish it: actions, words and thoughts. *Thoughts* come first and then *words* that reveal and manifest what the mind has conceived; last comes *action,* which puts into practice what one has thought. Perfection in Christian life consists in being fully like Christ, first in the inner heart and then in exterior action."[1]

Contemplation is, then, the set course for passing from communion with Christ in Mass to the imitation of Christ in life. Therefore, just as everyone in the Church is called to holiness,[2] we can equally talk of everyone in the Church being called to contemplation. The way to Christian perfection goes from the mysteries to contemplation and from contemplation to action. Together these three factors form one way to holiness, open to all Christians, according to the inscrutable degree of God's gift and man's free answer to it. In itself, the "primacy of contemplation" over action doesn't mean that contemplation is "greater" than the practice of the virtues and active life, but that it comes "first" — it is the source. This is especially true if we talk of a certain type of contemplation open to all and which all can practice.

1. *The constant memory of Christ*

As soon as we try to apply these general premises on the mysteries to the Eucharist, their importance and relevance is immediately obvious. The result is that to be like Christ it is not enough to eat his Body and drink his Blood; this mystery must be contemplated. There is a big affinity between the Eucharist and the incarnation. St. Augustine says that in the incarnation "Mary conceived the Word first in her mind and then in her body" (*Prius concepit mente quam corpore*). Actually, he adds, it would have been worth nothing to her to have carried Christ in her womb if she had not also carried him with love in her heart.[3]

54

After the incarnation, therefore, Mary was full of Jesus not only in her body but in her spirit too. She was full of Jesus because she thought of him and awaited him (and how she awaited him!); she loved Jesus. Like any woman expecting a child, but in a much more perfect way, she was more absorbed in what was happening within her than without, for within her was her treasure, the gentle secret that left her amazed and speechless. St. Luke tells us: "Mary kept all these things, pondering them in her heart" (Luke 2:19). In this she is the most perfect model of Eucharistic contemplation: that is what the Christians who have just received Jesus in the Eucharist must be like. They too must receive Jesus with their minds after receiving him into their bodies. And to receive Jesus with the mind means to think of him and have one's gaze fixed on him, to remember him. And here we have the key word of this meditation: to remember Jesus, to do things in memory of him.

These words were consecrated by Jesus when he said: "Do this in memory of me" (Luke 22:19). The word "memory" is what ideally connects the Eucharist to the Jewish Passover which, as we know, was also a "memorial" (cf. Exod 12:14). It is of such vital importance that St. Paul twice repeats this command of Jesus in his account of the institution of the Eucharist. He also specifies the content of this remembrance of Jesus: "As often as you eat this bread and drink the cup, you proclaim the Lord's death" (1 Cor 11:26). The content is Christ's death.

The Eucharistic memorial has a twofold significance: one concerns God and the other concerns humanity; we can therefore say it has a theological and an anthropological significance. In the *theological sense* the memorial consists in reminding the Father of Jesus — in inviting the Father to remember what Jesus did for us and, for his sake, to forgive us and help us. In short, we remind the Father of Jesus so that the Father will remember us. This is how a New Testament scholar explained the words of Jesus *Do this in memory of me:* "Do this that the Father may remember me." In the Old Testament, in moments of great trial, the people would turn to God, saying: "Remember, O Lord, in David's favor, all the hardships he endured" (Ps 132:1). But now we, the people of the New Covenant, can utter an infinitely more efficacious cry to God. We can say: Remember Jesus your Son, and his sacrifice! The Church Liturgy is our example in this. The Eucharistic Prayers of the Mass — and in particular Eucharistic

Prayer IV — are simply an *anamnesis,* or, a reminding the Father of Jesus. They relate with wonderful ingenuity (as if the Father didn't know!) what his Son said and did for us when he was on earth: "He gave himself up to death. . . . He sent the Holy Spirit from you, Father, as his first gift to those who believe. . . . He always loved those who were his own in the world. When the time came for him to be glorified by you, his heavenly Father, he showed the depth of his love. . . ." The words of consecration are narrative in style; they too are an account given to the Father of what Jesus said when he took bread and broke it for us. Only when the Father has been reminded at length of Jesus, do we pray the Father to remember us also: "Lord, remember those for whom we offer this sacrifice"; "Father, remember your Church."

In the *anthropological sense,* or existential, the Eucharistic memorial no longer consists in reminding the Father of Jesus but in reminding us of him. For many centuries, the first words uttered by the priest after the consecration were "Unde et memores. . . .": "Father, we celebrate the memory of Christ, your Son. We recall his passion, his resurrection from the dead, and his ascension into glory. . . ."[4] We must restore value to the immense spiritual potential enclosed in this memorial of Jesus. We must make the "sweet memory of Jesus" our joy and strength in this land of pilgrimage. "Jesus the very thought of Thee, with sweetness fills my breast. . . ." says an ancient liturgical hymn derived from St. Bernard.[5] We must reach the point of saying to Jesus what Isaiah said to God in the Old Testament: "Thy memorial name is the desire of our soul" (Isa 26:8). In fact, a flash of memory is able to catalyze our inner world and direct it towards the object, especially if this is a person and, moreover, one we love. When a mother thinks of her newborn baby, she does so in a transport of tenderness and maternal love. The same is true of the saints in a more spiritual way, when they think of God: "When I think of thee upon my bed, and meditate on thee in the watches of the night . . . in the shadow of thy wings I sing for joy" (Ps 63:6).

Memory is one of the most mysterious and splendid faculties of the human mind. Everything we have seen, heard, thought and done from our early infancy, is stored in this immense "womb," ready to be used at will. St. Augustine wrote some lovely things about memory which, for him, together with intelligence and will, was actually a sign and vestige of the Trinity: "Great is the power of memory, great indeed, God, a vast, a boundless inner room, whose depths none can reach . . . it is awesome in a way. . . . From when I first learned of you, you abide in my memory, and there I find you, whenever I recall you and take delight in you."[6] God, whom the heaven of heavens cannot hold is enclosed in the temple of human memory! The Latin word for "remember," *recordari,* (from which "record" derives with a different meaning), literally means to bring back again (*re-*) to the heart (*cor*). Therefore, it is not just an activity of the intellect, it is also one of the will and the heart; to remember is to think of with love. In fact, Jesus attributes the fact that we are able to "remember" him to the Holy Spirit (cf. John 14:26).

The Fathers of the Church and especially the Greek Fathers have elaborated a rich Eucharistic spirituality based on the words of Jesus and which are used in the liturgy: *Do this in memory of me.* For them, the spiritual fruit of the Eucharist is nothing else but the constant memory of Jesus. It is through this constant remembrance, in fact, that God comes to dwell in a soul and makes it his temple. According to St. Basil, Jesus instituted the Eucharist so that: "eating his Body and drinking his Blood, we would always remember him who died and rose again for us."[7]

However, the Fathers insist on one point: to effect a real transformation of our hearts, the contemplation of the mysteries must be "assiduous." "As grace-filled sorrow comes from love of Christ and love comes from thoughts of Christ and his love of mankind, it is of great help to conserve these thoughts in the memory and ceaselessly meditate on them in your heart. Moreover, this practice should be continuous, or, at least, frequent, throughout our whole life and never let anything interrupt it, so that these thoughts may become impressed in the mind and entirely possess the heart. As fire has to have continuous contact with an object to affect it, so an intermittent thought cannot bring about passion in a heart; a certain amount of time is necessary."[8]

Therefore, we must desire to reach the point where the memory of Jesus seeps into our minds and circulates there, like honey in a honeycomb. This is not an impossible undertaking and is within the reach of all Christians. Many souls, even those dwelling in the world, have lived this experience, at least for some periods of time. (We cannot surely expect to experience this memory permanently and stably in this life). It helps, especially at the beginning, to repeat a word mentally or with the lips — such as the prolonged invocation of the name Jesus. The efficacy of this simple means is almost incredible, for the name Jesus is not just a name; it encloses the mystery and power of the person of Christ. The invocation of the name Jesus helps, above all, to crush at the onset thoughts of pride, self-gratification, anger or impure thoughts and to develop, instead, good thoughts. All we have to do is observe our own thoughts as if they weren't ours and follow their development. It is clear straightaway where a certain thought is going to lead us — to God or to ourselves; whether it will result in his glory or ours. If this is the case, a repetition of the name Jesus with faith in the Lord's power will "break" the thread of the bad or useless thought and gradually instill into us "the mind which was in Christ Jesus" (Phil 2:5). In this way we can learn "to be on the side of God and not of human beings" (cf. Matt 16:23), and our hearts will become pure. What really spoils our heart is our self-seeking and the search for our own glory. Those who contemplate God turn away from themselves: they are obliged to forget themselves and lose sight of themselves. Those who contemplate God do not contemplate themselves!

2. *Adoration of the Most Holy Sacrament*

So far I have tried to highlight the general principle of Eucharistic contemplation and its place in the way to holiness. I should now like to mention the forms this may take and the means at our disposal to cultivate it.

An important form of Eucharistic contemplation is the *Liturgy of the Word* at Mass. This recalls each time an aspect of the history of salvation and an example from the life of Jesus, thereby adding something that is partly new to our memory of him. The Liturgy of the Word illuminates the Eucharist and helps us penetrate the endless depths of the mystery being celebrated. A practical example of this would be, let us say, the twenty-ninth Sunday, cycle B, of the liturgical year. The first reading we find is Isaiah 53:10-11: "Through his suffering my servant shall justify many, and their guilt he shall bear"; the second reading is Hebrews 4:14-16: "We have a great high priest. . . ."; and finally, the gospel passage from Mark 10:35-45: "Are you able to drink the cup that I drink? The Son of man also came not to be served . . . ." What horizons each of these verses opens to Eucharistic contemplation! The table of the Word prepares us for the table of the bread; it stirs desire and increases love for Christ. That is what happened in the extraordinary liturgy experienced by the two disciples of Emmaus. The Scriptures quoted by Jesus had made their hearts burn with longing so that they were able to "recognize" the Lord at the breaking of the bread.

Another form of Eucharistic contemplation is the time devoted to preparation and thanksgiving before and after Communion.

However, the highest form of Eucharistic contemplation is the silent adoration of the Blessed Sacrament. It is true that Jesus-Eucharist can be contemplated from afar, in the tabernacle of the mind. (St. Francis used to say: "When I don't hear Mass, I adore the Body of Christ in mental prayer; and I worship just as much as when I see it at Mass"[9]). Nevertheless, contemplation done in the real presence of Christ, before the species containing him, possibly in a quiet place filled, as it were, with his presence, is a great help to us.

In his letter of Holy Thursday 1980 on "The Mystery and Cult of the Most Holy Sacrament," Pope John Paul II, wrote: "The adoration of Christ in the Sacrament of Love must be expressed in different ways of Eucharistic devotion: personal prayer before the Blessed Sacrament, hours of adoration, and expositions that can be either short, long or yearly. . . . The animation and study of the Eucharistic cult are proof of the genuine renewal aimed at by the council and they are its central point. . . . Jesus awaits us in the Sacrament of Love. Let us find time to meet him in faith-filled adoration and contemplation." A reminder of this sort was necessary. Traditional Eucharistic devotion was, in fact, quite neglected in the fervor of liturgical renewal which, naturally, is more concerned with the community and ceremonial aspect than with personal devotion. It was also neglected through a certain naive, exaggerated, sociological and secular trend that saw only the convivial or, so to say, the horizontal aspect of the Eucharist. The centrifugal movement (towards the poor, politics, underdeveloped countries, etc.), which was characteristic of many Christian communities after the council, now needs to be counterbalanced by a centripetal movement to lead us back to the heart of the Church, where the Eucharist abides. The Archbishop of Milan, C. M. Martini, in his first pastoral letter "The Contemplative Dimension of Life," also insisted on the necessity of rediscovering the Eucharist: "All of this (making the Eucharist a way of life) requires, in practice, that we develop interior attitudes that precede, accompany and follow the Eucharistic celebration: listening to the revealed word, contemplation of the mysteries of Jesus, perception of the Father's will translucent in the words of Jesus, confrontation between the way of life that springs from the paschal and Eucharistic mystery and the ever new spiritual situations in which the community and single believers find themselves. In this, silent prayer, listening to the Word of God, meditation of Scripture, and personal reflection are not separate from the Eucharist but vitally connected to it."

Worship and adoration of the Eucharist outside Mass is relatively new in Christian devotion. In fact, it started to develop in the West at the beginning of the eleventh century as a reaction to the heresy of Berengar of Tours who denied the "real" presence, claiming that Jesus was only symbolically present in the Eucharist. Since then, however, we can say that there has not been a saint in whose life Eucharistic devotion has not been a determining factor. It has been the source of great spiritual energy, a sort of home fire that is always burning in God's house where all the great sons and daughters of the Church have warmed themselves.

Perhaps this relatively late development of Eucharistic worship outside Mass indicates that a certain freedom should be allowed to all Christian denominations on this point.[10] Eucharistic devotion is a gift of the Holy Spirit to the Catholic Church which she must gratefully cultivate for other Christians too, without, however, necessarily expecting them to do the same. Every important spiritual movement within Christianity has had its own particular charism to contribute to the richness of the whole Church. Protestants have the cult of God's Word; the Orthodox Church has the cult of icons (and what a lot we Catholics have received from them in this!). The Catholic Church has the Eucharist. The same fundamental aim is realized in all three ways — the contemplation of Christ and of his mystery.

If the gift that is peculiar to the Catholic Church and a secret of her strength lies in the unique way Jesus-Eucharist is present and adored in her, then it becomes obviously important that we should go back to fully appreciating this gift. It's as if the Holy Spirit were now urging the Church to practice again certain forms of Eucharistic devotion that have become somewhat outdated due to habit and a certain ritualism, but it must be done in a renewed way, infusing into it the growing biblical and liturgical riches that have meanwhile developed in Christian devotion. It is a time when there is great need for Eucharistic adoration and for staying, like Mary of Bethany, at the Master's feet (cf. Luke 10:39). We are rediscovering that the mystical body of Christ, the Church, can only live and develop around his real Body, the Eucharist.

In this sense I say the Eucharist makes the Church through contemplation. It is by staying still, in silence, and possibly for long periods, before Jesus in the Blessed Sacrament, that we perceive what he wants from us, put aside our own plans to make way for his, and let God's light gradually penetrate the heart and heal it. It's something like what happens to the trees in spring with the chlorophyll process. Green leaves sprout from the branches; these absorb certain elements from the air which, in the light of the sun, are "fixed" and become nourishment for the plant. Without these little green leaves the plant couldn't grow and bear fruit and would not contribute to regenerating the oxygen we ourselves breathe. We must be like those green leaves! They are a symbol of those Eucharistic souls who, contemplating the "Sun of Justice," Christ, "fix" the nourishment which is the Holy Spirit himself, to the benefit of the great tree, the Church. It is what St. Paul says in other words: "And we all, with unveiled face, beholding the glory of the Lord, are being changed into his likeness, from one degree of glory to another; for this comes from the Lord who is the Spirit" (2 Cor 3:18).

3. *I look at Him and He looks at me*

What is the precise meaning of Eucharistic contemplation? In itself, it is really the ability or better, the gift, of establishing a heart to heart contact with Jesus really present in the Host and, through him, of raising oneself to the Father in the Holy Spirit. All of this is done, as far as possible, in a state of outer and inner silence. Silence is the dearest spouse of contemplation; it protects it, as Joseph protected Mary. To contemplate is to intuitively fix the mind on the divine reality (this could be God himself, or one of his attributes, or a mystery in Christ's life) and relish his presence. In meditation the *search* for truth prevails while, in contemplation, *delight* in the found truth prevails.

Great spiritual masters have given us definitions of contemplation: "A free, penetrating and still gaze" (Hugh of St. Victor), or: "A loving look at God" (St. Bonaventure). In the parish of Ars there was once a peasant who used to pass hours in church, immobile, looking at the tabernacle, and when the Saint Curate of Ars asked him what he was doing there every day like that, he replied: "Nothing, I look at him and he looks at me!" This tells us that Christian contemplation is never a one-way gaze and neither is it directed at the "Nothing" (as in certain Oriental religions, in particular Buddhism). It is always the meeting of two looks; our look at God and God's look at us. If, at times, our gaze weakens, God's never does. Sometimes Eucharistic contemplation just means keeping Jesus company, being there under his gaze, giving him the joy of contemplating us, too. Although we are but useless creatures and sinners, we are still the fruit of his passion for whom he gave his life.

Eucharistic contemplation is not, therefore, hindered by any arid empty state that can be experienced, whether this is due to our own dissipation or permitted by God for our purification. We simply have to give it a meaning, even renouncing the satisfaction that fervor gives us, to praise God and say with Charles de Foucauld: "To please you, Jesus, that is all I want!"; that is to say: all I want is that you should be pleased. Jesus can dispose of eternity to make us happy — we have only this short space of time to make him happy. How could we resign ourselves to missing a chance that will never occur again for all eternity? At times Eucharistic adoration may simply seem to be a pure waste of time — we gaze and see nothing. Instead, what strength and proof of our faith it holds! Jesus knows we could leave and busy ourselves with a thousand other more gratifying things, but we stay there, simply giving him our time. When we cannot pray with our minds we can always do so with our bodies and that is prayer of the body (even if the mind is anything but absent).

In contemplating Jesus in the Sacrament of the altar, we actualize the prophecy made at the moment of Jesus's death on the Cross: "They shall look on him whom they have pierced" (John 19:37). This contemplation is itself a prophecy for it anticipates what we shall do forever in the heavenly Jerusalem. It is the most eschatological and prophetic act that can be done in the Church. In the end the Lamb will no longer be slain and his flesh will no longer be eaten. Consecration and Communion will cease, that is, but contemplation of the Lamb slain for us will not cease. This is precisely what the saints in heaven are doing (cf. Rev 5:1ff.). In front of the tabernacle we form one choir with the Church in heaven; they, as it were, facing the altar and with us behind it; they, face-to-face in the beatific vision, and we in faith.

"When Moses came down from Mount Sinai, he did not know that the skin of his face shone because he had been talking with God" (Exod 34:29). Moses did not know and neither shall we, (for it is well so). But maybe it will happen even to us after one of those moments, that someone will see our face shining because we have contemplated the Lord. It would indeed be the most wonderful gift we could give them.

NOTES

1. St. Gregory of Nyssa, *On the Ideal of Christian Perfection* (PG 46, 283f.).
2. Cf. Vatican II, *Lumen gentium* 39-40.
3. St. Augustine, *On the Sacred Virginity,* 3 (PL 40, 398).
4. *Eucharistic Prayer* I, ("*Roman Canon*").
5. Hymn *Jesu dulcis memoria.*
6. St. Augustine, *Confessions,* X, 8-24.
7. St. Basil the Great, *On Baptism* I, 3 (PG 31, 1576).
8. N. Cabasilas, *Life in Christ,* VI, 4 (PG 150, 653).
9. St. Francis of Assisi, *Writings and Early Biographies,* 1874).
10. Cf. M. Thurian, *Le Mystère de l'Eucharistie* (Presses de Taizé 1981) 62f.

Chapter Six

"I Have Given You An Example"

The Eucharist makes the Church through Imitation

In the Lukan and Pauline accounts of the Supper, we read the command of Jesus: "Do this in memory of me." Also in the Johannine account of the Last Supper we find a kind of command: "I have given you an example, that you also should do what I have done to you" (John 13:15). These two "commands" are undeniably related. Nevertheless, there is a difference: the first case is a question of "doing a memorial," and therefore refers to the liturgy; the second case is a question of doing ("that you also should do"), and refers to life. It is, therefore, the gospel sequence that encourages us to advance from memory to imitation, from Eucharistic contemplation to Eucharistic practice.

The Last Supper as described by John in chapters 13–17 of his Gospel is not a Passover meal. The Jewish Passover meal took place, in fact, on the evening of the 14 Nisan. (According to John, Jesus died on the 14 Nisan, before the Jews had partaken of the Passover meal and that is precisely why they did not enter Pilate's praetorium) (cf. John 18:28). The Passover meal of Jesus, described in the Synoptics, could have taken place a few days earlier, following a different liturgical calendar from the official one of the Temple and which the Essenes of Qumran also followed, unless it was the very same supper and the Synoptics just place emphasis on the Passover and Eucharistic aspect, whereas John makes no explicit mention of it.

The much discussed question of the chronology of the passion is not my concern here. It is sufficient to know why John doesn't relate the institution of the Eucharist in his account of the Last Supper and relates, instead, the washing of feet. It cannot be imagined that he was ignorant of the Eucharist or that it wasn't celebrated where the Fourth Gospel originated. On the contrary, it is known that, in the Fourth Gospel, the Eucharist is the liturgical setting in which the whole account of the Passover events

64

was shaped and took its "form." It is not even, as is usually believed, that John, who wrote his Gospel after the other evangelists, wanted to integrate the Synoptics and took what they already contained for granted, or that he simply didn't want to vulgarize the Christian mystery. The real reason is that, where the Passover and Eucharist are concerned, John clearly wants to stress the *event* more than the *sacrament,* or, the "signified" more than the sign. The new Passover didn't begin so much in the cenacle for him, when the commemorating *ritual* was instituted but on the cross when the *event* itself to be commemorated took place. In an analogous way, we might say that by giving importance to the washing of feet at the Last Supper, John wanted to remind the Christian community, which, by then, regularly celebrated the Eucharist, of the significance of this sacrament and the practical obligations it contained for the Church. The evangelist, as I said earlier on, tacitly urges us to pass from the liturgy to action, from memory to imitation.

1. *The significance of the washing of feet*

It is now obvious why it is so important to have a clear understanding of the significance the gesture of Jesus washing the apostles' feet held for John. It is another of those episodes (like, for example, the piercing of the side) where the evangelist implies the existence of a mystery far greater than the contingent fact which, in itself, might seem negligible.

Jesus said: "I have given you the example." What example was he referring to? Was it perhaps how to wash our brothers' feet every time we sit down to eat? It certainly was not! It was something else which is quite obvious to those who read the gospel and already know who Jesus is.

The account of the washing of feet has a deep affinity with the hymn of praise to Jesus in the Letter to the Philippians. This, too, is an invitation to imitate Christ: "Have this mind among yourselves, which was in Christ Jesus"; a description of Jesus follows who, though he was in the form of God, "emptied himself," taking the form of a servant. For his part, John presents Jesus to us who "knowing that the Father had given all things into his hands, and that he had come from God and was going to God," laid aside his garments, girded himself with a towel, (a servant's garment), and began to wash the disciples' feet. We could almost say that the evangelist is giving us through plastic images and practical facts what Paul says in general and explicit terms.

In fact, it is the theme that runs throughout the New Testament: Jesus, the servant of God and man. In Luke's Gospel, and precisely in the account of the Last Supper, there are words attributed to Jesus after he had washed his disciples' feet: "Which is the greater, one who sits at table, or one who serves? Is it not the one who sits at table? But I am among you as one who serves" (Luke 22:27). According to the evangelist, Jesus said this because of a dispute that had arisen among them as to which of them was to be regarded as the greatest (cf. Luke 22:24). Perhaps it was the same situation that inspired Jesus to wash their feet, like a live parable. While the disciples were discussing animatedly among themselves, in silence he rose from table, searched for a basin of water and a towel and went back and knelt before Peter to wash his feet, understandably causing him great embarrassment: "Lord, do you wash my feet?" (John 13:6).

With the washing of feet, it's as if Jesus were summarizing the meaning of his life to impress it on the disciples' minds so that when the time came for them to understand, they would do so: "What I am doing you do not know now, but afterward you will understand" (John 13:7). Placed at the conclusion of the Gospels, this action tells us that the whole of the life of Jesus from beginning to end, was a washing of feet, and that is to say, a service to humanity. It was, as some exegetes like to say, a *pro-existence,* or a life lived for others.

Jesus gave us the example of a life lived for others, a life become "broken bread for the world," as the theme of the World Eucharistic Congress held some years ago in Lourdes rightly declared. With the words: "Do as I have done," Jesus therefore instituted the *diakonia,* service, raising it to a fundamental law or better, to a way of life and model of all relations within the Church.

Jesus had told Peter that he would understand "afterward" and, indeed, afterward — after Easter — the Church never stops talking about service and inculcating it into the disciples in every way possible. When presenting the real widow, the Pastoral Epistles mention the washing of feet as a necessary factor: "She must have washed the feet of the saints . . ." (1 Tim 5:10). Even the doctrine on charisms is directed towards service, which is clearly the spirit and aim of each charism. St. Paul states that each "manifestation of the Spirit" is given "for the common good" (cf. 1 Cor 12:7) and that his gifts were given "to knit God's people together for a work of service" (*diakonia*) (cf. Eph 4:12). St. Peter, too, when he recommends hospitality, says: "As each has received a gift (charism), employ it for one another" (1 Pet 4:10). The two things — charism and ministry, or service — seem to be intrinsically related. A charism that is not expressed in service is like a talent hidden in the ground and becomes a source of condemnation (cf. Matt 25:25). It is like an unused plough growing rusty. The Church is charismatic to serve!

2. *The spirit of service*

We must closely examine the significance of "service" if it is not to remain just a mere word in our lives. In itself, service is not a virtue; in no list of virtues or fruits of the Holy Spirit, as the New Testament defines them, do we find the word *diakonia,* service. Actually, mention is made of a service to sin (cf. Rom 6:16) or to idols (cf. 1 Cor 6:9) which is, undoubtedly, not good. Service is neutral in itself: it indicates a way of living or a way of relating to others in one's work; being at the dependence of others. It can even be negative if done under constraint (slavery), or simply out of interest. Service is much discussed today: everyone is in service: a shopkeeper serves his customers; anyone who works is said to be in service. Evidently the gospel speaks of a very different kind of service, even if it doesn't necessarily exclude or disqualify service in worldly terms. The difference lies in the reason for the service and in the inner attitude with which it is carried out. Let us read once more the account of the washing of the feet to see with what spirit Jesus did it and what prompted him to do it: "Having loved his own who were in the world, he loved them to the end" (John 13:1). Service is not a virtue but it springs from virtue, especially from charity; actually it is the greatest expression of the new commandment. Service is a manifestation of the *agape,* or of a love that "does not insist on its own interests" (cf. 1 Cor 13:5), but on that of others; it does not consist in self-seeking but in giving. It is, all told, participating in and imitating God's way of acting who, because he is "Good, all Good and the supreme Good," cannot but love and help us freely and disinterestedly. This is why evangelical service, unlike that of the world, is not recommended to those who are inferior, to the needy and the poor but to those who have much, those in high places, the rich. Every one to whom much is given, of him will much be required where service is concerned (cf. Luke 12:48). That's why Jesus says that in his Church, the *leader* must become *one who serves* (Luke 22:26) and whoever is *first* must become *the slave of all* (Mark 10:44). The washing of the feet is "the sacrament of Christian authority" (C. Spicq).

Besides gratuity, service is the expression of another aspect of divine *agape:* humility. The words Jesus said, "You also ought to wash one another's feet," mean: you must offer one another the service of humble charity. Charity and humility together form evangelical service. Jesus once said: "Learn from me for I am gentle and humble of heart" (Matt 11:29). What had Jesus done to call himself "humble"? Had he, perhaps, thought lowly of himself or spoken unassumingly about himself? He had done quite the opposite! During the actual washing of the feet he called himself "Teacher and Lord" (cf. John 13:13). What had he done, therefore, to call himself "humble"? He humbled himself; he came down from heaven to serve! And from the moment of the incarnation he continued to come down to the point of kneeling down to wash his apostles' feet. How the angels must have shuddered to see the Son of God humble himself so, he upon whom they do not even dare to look (cf. 1 Pet 1:12). The Creator kneeling before his creatures! "Proud ashes, blush with shame. God humbles himself and you exalt yourself!" St. Bernard used to say to himself.[1] Seen like this — as humbling oneself to serve — humility is indeed a regal way of being like God and of imitating the Eucharist in our lives. "Look at God's humility, my brothers," St. Francis exclaimed, "and pour out your hearts before him. Humble yourselves so that you may be exalted by him. Keep nothing for yourselves, so that he who has given himself wholly to you may receive you wholly."[2]

The fruit of this meditation should be a courageous examination of our lives (our habits, position, schedule, distribution and use of our time) to see if it is really a service and if love and humility are part of it. The important thing to know is whether we are serving our brothers and sisters or whether, instead, they are serving our purposes. We make others serve our purpose or we take advantage of them, perhaps even when we are doing our utmost for them, if we are not disinterested and are, in some way, seeking approval, applause or the satisfaction of having a clear conscience, of being the benefactor. The gospel requirements are extremely radical on this point: "Do not let your left hand know what your right hand is doing" (Matt 6:3). Everything we do "to be noticed by others" is lost. "Christ did not please himself!" (Rom 15:3): this is the rule of service.

To have a "discernment of spirits" or of our intentions in doing service, we should be aware of what we do willingly and what we do our best to shirk. We should see if our heart is ready to abandon a noble, prestigious service, if required, for a humble unappreciated one. The surest service we can give is that which is hidden from the eyes of all except the Father's, who sees into our secret hearts. Jesus raised the washing of feet, one of the most humble acts of his time as it was usually done by slaves, to a symbol of service. St. Paul warns us: "Do not be haughty, but associate with the lowly" (Rom 12:16).

The opposite to a spirit of service is the wish to domineer, the habit to enforce our wills, our points of view and ways, on others. In a word, authoritarianism. Often a person of tyrannical disposition doesn't even realize the suffering he causes and is almost amazed at how little his "concern" and efforts are appreciated. He even becomes the victim. Jesus told his apostles to be like "lambs among wolves," but such a person is like a wolf among lambs. Much of the suffering that families and communities are often subjected to is due to the presence of an authoritarian and despotic person who tramples on others with nailed boots, as it were, and under the pretext of "serving" others, actually takes advantage of them.

This "someone" might possibly well be us! If we have the slightest doubt about this, we should sincerely consult those we live with and give them the opportunity to express themselves frankly. If it results that our way of behaving makes life difficult for someone, we should humbly accept the fact and reflect on our service.

In another way, being too attached to our habits and comfort also goes against the spirit of service — a spirit of laxness, as it were. It is not possible to seriously serve others if we are constantly intent on pleasing ourselves, making an idol out of our rest, our free time, our schedule. The rule of service is always the same: "Christ did not please himself."

We have seen that service is the virtue of those in charge. Jesus left it as a treasure to the pastors of his Church. We have seen that all the charisms are given for the purpose of service, but particularly the charism of "pastors and teachers" (cf. Eph 4:11), the charism of authority. The Church is "charismatic" to serve and it is also "ministerial" to serve!

3. Service of the Spirit

If, for all Christians, to serve means "living no longer for themselves" (cf. 2 Cor 5:15), for pastors it means: "not feeding themselves": "Ho, shepherds of Israel, who have been feeding themselves! Should not shepherds feed the sheep? (Ezek 34:2). Nothing appears more natural and right to people than that whoever is lord (*dominus*) should "dominate," act, as it were, as lord. But this is "not the way" for the disciples of Jesus; whoever is lord must serve. "Not that we lord it over your faith," writes St. Paul, "we work with you for your joy" (2 Cor 1:24). The Apostle Peter recommends the same thing to pastors: "Do not dominate over those in your charge but be an example to the flock" (cf. 1 Pet 5:3). It is not easy in pastoral ministry to avoid the mentality of being a lord of the faith, which became part of the concept of authority very early on. In one of the most ancient documents on episcopal authority, we find the idea that a bishop is like a monarch, in whose Church nothing can be undertaken without his consent.

Where pastors are concerned and in so far as they are pastors, this point is often the decisive factor in conversion. How strong and sad the words Jesus uttered after the washing of the feet sound: "I, your Lord and Master . . . !" "Jesus did not count equality with God a thing to be grasped" (Phil 2:6), and that is to say, he wasn't afraid of compromising his divine dignity, of fostering people's disrespect by disregarding his own privileges and appearing as one among us. Jesus led a simple life; simplicity has always been the beginning and the sign of a genuine return to the gospel. We must imitate God's way of acting. Nothing, Tertullian wrote, better portrays God's way of acting so much as the contrast between the simplicity of the ways and means with which he works and the magnificence of the spiritual results obtained.[3] The world needs a great display to act and impress, but God doesn't. There was a time when the dignity of bishops was seen in insignia, titles, castles, armies. They were, so to speak, prince-bishops, and sometimes much more prince than bishop. Today seems like a golden time for the Church in comparison. I know a bishop who often finds it natural to pass a few hours in an old people's home, helping them to dress and eat; he has taken the washing of feet literally. Personally, I have received wonderful examples of simplicity in my life from prelates.

It is necessary, however, to maintain a sense of evangelic freedom on this point too. Simplicity necessitates that we do not place ourselves above others but neither should we obstinately always place ourselves beneath them to somehow keep our distance, but that, in the things of ordinary routine we accept to be like others. Manzoni makes a sharp observation when he says there are those who have all the humility necessary when it comes to placing themselves beneath others but not when it is a question of being their equals.[4] At times, the best service is not in serving but in accepting to be served, like Jesus who, at the right moment, knew how to sit at table and let another wash his feet (cf. Luke 7:38) and who willingly accepted the provisions made for him on his journeys by the generous and loving women (Luke 8:2-3).

Where pastoral service, or pastors, are concerned we must not forget that service to the brethren, no matter how important and holy, is not the first or essential thing; service to God comes first. Jesus is first and foremost the "Servant of God" and then the servant of humanity. He even reminds his parents of this when he says: "Did you not know that I must be about my Father's house?" (Luke 2:49). He never hesitated to delude the crowds that had gathered to hear him and be healed of infirmities when he unexpectedly withdrew to the wilderness to pray (cf. Luke 5:16). Today, even evangelical service is endangered by the risk of secularization. It can all too easily be taken for granted that all service to humanity is God's service. St. Paul speaks of a service of the Spirit (*diakonia Pneumatos*) (2 Cor 3:8), to which the ministers of the New Testament are destined. In pastors, the spirit of service must be expressed in service of the Spirit!

Those, like priests, who are called by vocation to a "spiritual" service, do not serve their brethren by doing all sorts of things for them and then neglecting the only thing the brethren rightfully expect from them and which only they can render. It is written that a priest "is appointed to act on behalf of people in relation to God" (Heb 5:1). When this problem arose for the first time in the Church, Peter solved it like this: "It is not right that we should give up preaching the word of God to serve tables. . . . We will devote ourselves to prayer and to the ministry of the Word" (Acts 6:2-4). In fact, there are pastors who have taken up serving tables again. They busy themselves with all sorts of problems, whether they be problems of money, administration or even agriculture, that exist in their communities (even when these could quite easily be seen to by others), and they neglect their real ministry, which cannot be delegated. The ministry of the Word requires hours of reading, study and prayer. The Church community generally complains today that preaching is inadequate and devoid of content. Many of the faithful come out from Mass indignant at the homily and feeling more arid and empty than ever. I am convinced that this is the first pastoral problem in order of importance. We must say, with Isaiah: "The poor and needy seek water and there is none" (Isa 41:17). The people seek bread and, often, they receive empty and trite words which hold no sense of God; or they receive nothing at all.

What St. Gregory the Great said is still very relevant today: "There are too few workers for such a big harvest and we are profoundly saddened by this, for many would listen to the good news but preachers are scarce. True, the world is full of priests and yet it is hard to find workers for the Lord's vineyard. We have entered the state of priesthood but do not do what this state involves. We have become engrossed in worldly affairs which have nothing to do with the priestly state. We who neglect the ministry of preaching are still called bishops, and maybe this is to our judgement for we possess the honorary title but not the qualities. . . . The more we concern ourselves with worldly affairs, the more indifferent we become interiorly."[5]

4. *Service to the poor*

It is now opportune to concern ourselves with an important aspect of service in the Church, relevant to both priests and laity alike. I am referring to service to the poor. In his First Letter, John the evangelist writes: "He laid down his life for us; and we ought to lay down our lives for the brethren. But if one has the world's goods and sees his brother in need, yet closes his heart against him, how does God's love abide in him? Little children, let us not love in words or speech but in deed and in truth" (1 John 3:16-18). St. Augustine said that with these words, "the blessed Apostle John clearly intended to explain the mystery of the Lord's Supper to us."[6] In John's mind, therefore, this is an essential aspect of the Eucharistic mystery.

A simple line of theological reasoning gives us the key to all of this. Jesus Christ, whose Body and Blood are consecrated, and whom we receive and adore in the Blessed Sacrament of the altar is, according to Church dogma, "true God and true man." Now, we acknowledge and proclaim Jesus as "true God" in Eucharistic adoration, which we have dealt with in the previous chapter. But how and in what way do we actually proclaim our faith in Jesus as "true man"? Precisely by ministering to the poor and suffering! Therefore, adoration is an essential aspect of the Eucharistic mystery but it is not sufficient; sharing must be added to adoration. He who held the bread and said: *This is my body!*, was saying it also of the poor. He said it when, on speaking of what had been done for the hungry, the thirsty, the prisoner and the naked, he solemnly declared: *You did it to me!;* when, identifying himself totally with them, he said: *I* was hungry, *I* was thirsty, *I* was a stranger, *I* was naked, sick, in prison (cf. Matt 25:35ff.).

Christ's presence in the poor and hungry is not the same kind of presence as in the bread and wine on the altar; it is, however, a "real" presence, a true presence, and not fictitious or imaginary, because Jesus identified himself with them. He "instituted" this symbol of the poor just as he instituted the Eucharist. We might say that Christ is passively, and not actively, present in the poor. In fact, the poor do not necessarily always have Christ in them and transmit him to those that welcome them as the Eucharistic species do. They are not "efficacious signs of grace," as the sacrament is; they do not produce grace in themselves or, as theology tells us, "ex opere operato." So one could "give away all he has" as St. Paul says, and it would gain him nothing, if he has not charity (cf. 1 Cor 13:3). Yet, he who refuses to welcome the poor with whom Christ identified himself, does not wholly welcome Christ. The great philosopher and believer, B. Pascal, during his last illness, when he was no longer able to keep down what he swallowed and the holy Viaticum was deferred, as "he could not communicate with the Head," he asked for the company of some poor persons beside his bed, so as, he said, "to communicate at least with the body."[7] Mother Teresa of Calcutta said: "If we can see Jesus under the species of bread, we can also see him in the mutilated bodies of the poor. We need the poor to see him."

St. Leo the Great used to say that, after the ascension of Jesus into heaven, "all that was visible in our Lord Jesus Christ is now seen in the sacramental symbols in the Church."[8] This principle which, where St. Leo was concerned, applied to the sacraments and ministries of the Church, including his pontifical ministry, applies in another sense to the poor and all those whom Jesus calls "the least of my brethren" (Matt 25:40). Since the ascension, all that was humanly visible in Christ is now seen in the poor and suffering who are his living representatives. In fact, if by the incarnation, every person — as certain Fathers of the Church loved to say — has been somehow assumed by the Word, it is the poor, the suffering and rejected that have been very particularly taken up by the Word, due to the *way* in which the incarnation came about. Jesus could actually have been born and lived a rich life, honored and glorious, yet he chose to be born and live poor, suffering and despised. The incarnation attests that the Word became man, but the paschal mystery attests what kind of man the Word had become: a man who was defenseless, condemned, and crucified.

In a well-known discourse, St. John Chrysostom stressed the close connection that exists between Jesus present on the altar and Jesus present in the poor: "Do you," he asks, "wish to honor the Body of Christ? Then do not allow it to be scorned in its members, in the poor, who have nothing to clothe themselves with. Do not honor him in church with silk and then neglect him outside when he is cold and naked. . . . What does Christ gain from a sacrificial table full of golden vessels when he then dies of hunger in the persons of the poor? First of all feed the hungry and only then dress the altar with what is left. Would you offer him a golden chalice and refuse him a glass of water? What need is there to dress his altar with gold, if then you fail to offer him some necessary clothing? . . . Therefore, while you adorn the place of worship, do not lock your heart to your suffering brother. This is a more precious living temple than the other."[9]

Today, the duty to honor Christ in the poor asserts itself in a different way. It is not a question of giving alms to the first one that asks you; in many cases this has become a serious problem and, anyhow, it is not enough. It is, above all, a question of opening our eyes to the scandalous injustice in the world where less than *twenty* per cent of the world population (roughly what corresponds to the rich and Christian peoples in the northern countries) consumes more than *eighty* per cent of the earth's resources. I am of the opinion that, just as in medieval times great popes and saints traveled all over the Christian world to organize the crusades, so today, we must pray God for something similar to happen, a sort of mass mobilization of all Christianity for a new crusade: a crusade to free the thousands and thousands of Christ's living temples who are dying of hunger, disease and misery. Therefore, no longer Christ's empty tomb and the places he walked, but his living tombs where he lies and suffers. This would be a "crusade" worthy of the name, worthy, that is, of the crucifix!

To St. Paul the fact that "one is hungry and another is drunk" is an impediment for receiving the Eucharist. "When you meet together" — he wrote to the Corinthians — "it is not the Lord's supper that you eat. For in eating, each one goes ahead with his own meal, and one is hungry and another is drunk" (1 Cor 11:20-21). To say that "it is not the Lord's supper that you eat" is the same as saying that this is no longer Eucharist. This is a very strong assertion, also from a theological point of view, to which, perhaps, we do not give due attention. Now the situation where "one is hungry and another is drunk" is no longer a local problem but a world-wide one. There can be no similarity between the Lord's supper and the supper the rich man gave where they feasted lavishly, forgetting the poor man outside the door (cf. Luke 16:19ff.). The longing to share something with those in need, both near and far, must be an integral part of our devotion and Eucharistic life. There is no one who, if he wishes, cannot during the week do one of the deeds Jesus listed and of which he says: "You did it to me!" Sharing, in fact, is not just "giving" (bread, clothes, a house); it is also "visiting" (a prisoner, someone sick, an old person who is lonely . . .). It is not just giving money but also one's time. The poor and suffering are not in less need of solidarity and love than bread and clothes to clothe themselves with. Jesus said: "You always have the poor with you but you will not always have me" (Matt 26:11). This is true also in the sense that we cannot always receive the Body of Christ in the Eucharist and, even when we do receive it, it lasts only a few seconds, whereas we can always receive him in the poor. There are no limits, all that is required is to want it. The poor are always near at hand. Every time we are close to someone suffering, particularly when extreme suffering is present, we should hear, with ears of faith, the voice of Christ repeating: "This is my body!"

When he had just explained the significance of the washing of the feet to the apostles, Jesus said to them: "If you know these things, blessed are you if you do them" (John 13:17). We too will be blessed if we do not content ourselves with knowing these things — that the Eucharist prompts us to service and sharing — but if we do them, beginning possibly today. Yes, the Eucharist is not only a mystery to consecrate, to receive, to contemplate and adore. It is also a mystery to imitate.

NOTES

1. St. Bernard, *Praises of the Virgin Mother,* I, 8.
2. St. Francis of Assisi, *Letter to a General Chapter,* 2 (*Writings,* 106).
3. Tertullian, *On Baptism,* 1 (CCL 1, 277).
4. A. Manzoni, *The Betrotheds,* ch. 38.
5. St. Gregory the Great, *Homilies on the Gospels* 17, 3 (PL 76, 1139f.).
6. St. Augustine, *Sermon* 304, 1 (PL 38, 1395).
7. Cf. *Life of B. Pascal,* written by his Sister Gilberte.
8. St. Leo the Great, *Sermon 2 on the Ascension,* 2 (PL 54, 398).
9. St. John Chrysostom, *Homily* 50, 3-4 (PG 58, 508f.).

Chapter Seven

"Behold, Something Greater Than Solomon Is Here"

The Eucharist as the real presence of the Lord

I began these reflections with the Eucharist in the history of salvation; in it we saw the mystery of the Eucharist present in different ways in the entire history of salvation; as a *figure* in the Old Testament, as an *event* in the New Testament and as a *sacrament* in the Church today. I then dwelt on the Eucharist as sacrament and how it "makes" the Church through consecration, communion, contemplation and imitation. In these last chapters I should like to move back again to the beginning — to the Eucharist in the history of salvation, with an eye, however, to the present and the future. St. Thomas asserts that the Christian mystery is always three-dimensional: *memory* of the past, *presence* of grace and *expectation* of eternal fulfillment.[1] For this reason he calls the Eucharist "the sacred banquet in which Christ is received as food, the memory of his passion is recalled, the mind is filled with grace and we are given a pledge of our future glory."[2]

We shall now consider the Eucharist as the real presence of the Lord in the Church and, in the next chapter, the Eucharist as waiting for the Lord's coming.

1. *"Behold, the dwelling of God with us!"*

One summer's day, I was celebrating Mass in a convent. The gospel passage was Matthew 12. I shall never forget the impression these words of Jesus made on me: "Behold, something greater than Jonah is here. . . . Something greater than Solomon is here." Surely I was hearing them for the first time! I understood that the word "here" really meant here, in this precise place, at this precise moment, and not only when Jesus was on earth many centuries ago. A shudder ran through me and I was shaken out of my torpor: right there in front of me was something greater than Jonah, something greater than Solomon, than Abraham, than Moses: there was the Son of the living God! I understood the meaning of the words: "Lo, I am with you always . . ." (Matt 28:20).

Ever since that summer's day, these words have become dear and familiar to me in a new way. Very often during Mass, when I genuflect after the consecration I say to myself: "Behold, something greater than Jonah is here! Something greater than Solomon is here!" As I wish now to reflect on the real presence of Jesus in the Eucharist, I could not think of more suitable words to start with and keep in mind during this reflection.

However, before becoming immersed in the mystery of the real presence in the Eucharist, let us pause on the threshold for a moment and look, from outside as it were, at the background setting of the whole Bible. In this overall picture, the real presence in the Eucharist appears as the natural conclusion of biblical revelation on God, like the final touch to a canvas, that reveals God's true countenance to us. Biblical God is a God-with-us, a God who is present and not a God who is "nonexistent in human matters," and beyond reach like the God of philosophers. That is why God fully and finally manifests himself in the Eucharist. The Eucharist is really the burning bush where God reveals himself as Yahweh, that is as the one "who *is there,* who is *present,*" close at hand for his people (cf. Exod 3:14).

Isaiah continues in this line when he talks of a child who will be called Immanuel, God-with-us (cf. Isa 7:14). And finally the event that fulfills all these promises: "The Word became flesh and dwelt among us" (John 1:14). God's presence which up to now had been manifested in a cloud of glory — an elusive glory that came and went — now manifests itself in visible, touchable flesh permanently with us.

We have heard, seen with our eyes, looked upon and touched with our hands the Word of life! (cf. John 1:1). In this striking list of participles: heard, seen, looked upon, touched, there is still one missing: eaten. This final step takes place with the institution of the Eucharist: "Take and eat. . . ."; "He who eats my flesh will have eternal life." God's universal and, we might say, external presence, has now become personal and interior in us, and not just in an intentional and spiritual way (as happens in seeing, in listening, in contemplation and in faith) but in a real way, totally adapted to our human condition. The Eucharist is the last step in the long path of God's "condescension": creation, revelation, incarnation, Eucharist. Quite rightly, on the feast of "Corpus Christi," the liturgy used to apply these words of Moses to the Eucharist: "For what great nation is there that has a God so near to it as the Lord our God is to us?" (Deut 4:7). In front of the tabernacle we can truthfully repeat these words from Revelation: "Behold, the dwelling of God is with us!" (Rev 21:3). The Eucharist is related to the Easter mystery but it is equally related to the incarnation. It is the *memorial of a happening* — passion and resurrection — but it is also the *presence of a person:* the incarnate Word. In the passage from the first to the sixth chapter of his Gospel, St. John highlights this affinity: the Word became flesh (incarnation) and the flesh became "true bread" (Eucharist). The eternal life that was made manifest to us in the incarnation (cf. 1 John 1:2), is now given to us to eat, it has become the "bread of eternal life." The Eucharist draws its infinite divine power from the fact that it puts us into contact with the flesh of the God-Man.

2. *"Hold fast what is good"*

Let us now cross over the threshold. Let us go beyond the veil and enter the bright cloud, the "Holy of Holies." In other words, let us tackle the mystery of the real presence of Jesus in the Eucharist. How can we deal with such a deep and incomprehensible mystery? Memories of the numerous theories and discussions on it, the dissensions between Catholics and Protestants, between the Latin and Orthodox Churches, which filled our theology books at one time, assail us. All of which makes it seem impossible to add anything to this mystery that might edify our faith and warm our hearts, without inevitably slipping into interdenominational polemics. And yet this is the wonder being worked by the Holy Spirit today among all Christians. He is prompting us to admit to what extent our Eucharistic disputes were based on the human presumption that this mystery could be enclosed in a theory, or even in a word, and on the will to prevail over our adversaries. He is prompting us to repent for having reduced the supreme pledge of love and unity left to us by Our Lord to our favorite topic of discussion.

The way to Eucharistic ecumenism is the way to mutual recognition, the Christian way of *agape,* or sharing. We are not asked to ignore the real differences that exist or to break faith with any point of authentic Catholic doctrine. It is a question of bringing together the positive aspects and authentic values in every tradition so as to form a "mass" of common truths that will gradually lead us to unity. It is unbelievable how some Catholic, Orthodox and Protestant points of view on the real presence appear to be so divergent and destructive whenever they are seen in contrast or as alternatives, and how they appear wonderfully convergent when they are carefully brought together. We must therefore set about making a synthesis. We must, as it were, sift the great Christian traditions to take out what is not good and, as St. Paul exhorts us, to "hold fast what is good" (cf. 1 Thess 5:21). If we put things together in this way, what is from God will remain and what is from man will be eliminated.

3. *A real but hidden presence: the Catholic tradition*

In this spirit, let us now take a close look at the three main Eucharistic traditions — Catholic, Orthodox and Protestant — to be edified by the treasures they contain and unite them in the common treasure of the Church. As a result we shall find that our understanding of the mystery of the real presence is richer and more vivid. In Catholic theology, the consecration is the indisputable heart of the Eucharist, from which we have Christ's real presence. At the consecration, Jesus himself acts and speaks. On this point, Western theology is influenced by a whole trend in patristic tradition. For example, St. Ambrose wrote: "The bread is bread before the sacramental words are pronounced. . . . Which words make the consecration effective and whose words are they? They belong to the Lord Jesus! Everything said before that moment is said by the priest who praises God, prays for the people, for the king and others. But when it is time for the venerable sacrament to be effected, the priest no longer uses his own words, but Christ's. Therefore, it is the words that work (*conficit*) the sacrament. . . . See how efficacious (*operatorius*) are Christ's words. The body of Christ was not present before the consecration but after it the body of Christ is present. For he spoke and it came to be, he commanded and it stood forth (cf. Ps 33:9)."[3]

From the Western Catholic viewpoint we can talk of a *Christological realism*. "Christological" because attention is centered on Christ seen both in his historical and incarnate state and as the Risen One. Christ is both the object and subject of the Eucharist, and that is to say, he is fulfilled in the Eucharist and he fulfills the Eucharist. "Realism" because Jesus is not seen as present on the altar simply in a sign or symbol (contrary to what Berengar of Tours said), but in truth and in his reality. This Christological realism is clear, for example, in the hymn "Ave Verùm," composed by Pope Innocent IV for the elevation of the Host. It says:

> "Hail to thee! true body, sprung
> From the Virgin Mary's womb!
> The same that on the cross was hung,
> And bore for man the bitter doom.
> Thou whose side was pierced and flow'd
> Both with water and with blood. . . ."

Later on, the Council of Trent gave a more precise explanation of this approach to the real presence. Three adverbs were used: *vere, realiter, substantialiter.* Jesus is *truly* present and not simply through image or form, he is *really* present, and not only subjectively through the faith of believers; he is *substantially* present, that is, in his profound reality, which cannot be seen by the senses, and not in the appearances which remain that of bread and wine.

It is true that the risk of falling into a "crude" or exaggerated realism existed, almost as if — as a formula contrasting Berengar's heresy stated — the Body and Blood of Christ were "sensitively present on the altar and were indeed touched and broken by the priest's hands and masticated by the faithful."[4] The remedy to this risk is to be found in tradition itself. St. Augustine made it clear, once and for all, that the presence of Jesus in the Eucharist is "in the sacrament." In other words, it is a sacramental and not a physical presence, mediated by signs, and precisely, by bread and wine. However, in this case the *sign* does not exclude the *reality* but makes it present to us, in the only way in which the risen Christ, living "in the Spirit," can be present to us as long as we are on this earth.

Another great master of Western Eucharistic spirituality, St. Thomas Aquinas, says the same thing when he talks about Christ's presence "in substance" under the species of bread and wine.[5] In fact, to say that Jesus is substantially present in the Eucharist, is to say that he is present in his true reality which nourishes us only through faith. In the *Adoro te devote,* attributed to the same St. Thomas, we sing:

> "Sight, touch, and taste in thee are each deceived;
> The ear alone most safely is believed."

In the opening strophe this same hymn originally develops Augustine's sacramental vision saying that Christ is present in the Eucharist through the species, or forms:

> "O Godhead hid, devoutly I adore thee,
> Who truly art within the forms before me."

The Latin expression "vere latitas" is charged with meaning; it means: you are hidden but truly there (the accent being in this case on "vere," on the reality of his presence) and it also means: you are truly there but hidden (the accent being here on "latitas," on the sacramental character of this presence). Thus the danger of "crude" realism is overcome. In another of his Eucharist hymns, St. Thomas says that they who partake of Christ,

> "Sever not, nor rend, nor break,
> But entire their Lord receive."[6]

Jesus is therefore present in the Eucharist in a totally unique way. No single word can suitably describe this presence, not even the adjective "real." The word real is derived from *res* (thing) and means, as a thing or an object. But Jesus is not present in the Eucharist as a "thing" or an object, but as a person. If we really want to name this presence, it would be better to simply say "Eucharistic" presence, because it occurs only in the Eucharist.

4. *The action of the Holy Spirit: the Orthodox Tradition*

The Western theology is very rich but it is not, nor could it be, exhaustive. In the past, at least, the importance due to the Holy Spirit and essential to an understanding of the Eucharist was neglected. And so we turn to the East to see what the Orthodox tradition has to offer us. However, our attitude today is different; we are no longer worried about the differences but grateful for what is offered to help complete our own views. In fact, the Orthodox tradition has always given great importance to the action of the Holy Spirit in Eucharistic celebration. Since Vatican Council II, this sharing has already shown results. Up to then, the Roman Canon of the Mass only mentioned the Holy Spirit incidentally in the final doxology: "Through him, with him, in him . . . in the unity of the Holy Spirit . . . ." Now, instead, all the new canons have a double invocation to the Holy Spirit: one on the gifts before the consecration and another on the Church after the consecration.

Oriental liturgies have always attributed the actual real presence of Christ on the altar to the particular action of the Holy Spirit, and this to the point of seeing the epiclesis, that is the invocation of the Spirit, and not the consecration, as the precise moment when Christ's presence is produced. In the "anaphora of St. James," in use in the Antiochian Church, the Holy Spirit is invoked with these words: "Send forth upon us and upon these gifts, your most Holy Spirit, Lord and giver of life, who reigns with you, God the Father, and with your only Son. He reigns consubstantially and co-eternally; he spoke through the law and the prophets and the New Testament; he descended in the form of a dove upon our Lord Jesus Christ in the river Jordan; he descended upon the Apostles on the day of Pentecost, in the form of tongues of fire. Send, O Lord, your thrice Holy Spirit upon us and upon these gifts, so that by his holy, gracious and glorious coming, he may sanctify this bread and make it into the sacred Body of Christ (Amen), and sanctify this chalice and make it into the precious Blood of Christ (Amen)."

This is much more than a simple addition to the invocation to the Holy Spirit. It is a wide-ranging and penetrating look at the history of salvation that opens a new dimension on the Eucharistic mystery. Starting with the words of the Nicene Constantinople Creed which define the Holy Spirit as "Lord and giver of life . . .

who spoke through the prophets," the perspective then widens to outline a real "history" of the Holy Spirit. He has always acted where life is given. At the beginning of time Adam was just an inertial mass of mud, but it received "the breath of life" and became a living being. When it was time for the New Adam to come, the Holy Spirit again intervened with Mary to create the life of the Saviour in her. In the cenacle we find a handful of frightened and doubtful men, a sort of inert body, like that of the first human being; then the Spirit breathed on them and they became the living Church. It is through the Spirit that the leap in quality into life and the history of salvation takes place each time.

The Eucharist brings this series of wonderful events to fulfillment. The Holy Spirit, who at Easter bursts into the sepulcher, "touches" Christ's Body and gives him life again, repeats this wonder in the Eucharist. He comes upon the dead elements of bread and wine and gives them life; he makes them into the Body and Blood of the Redeemer. Truly, as Jesus himself says of the Eucharist, "it is the Spirit that gives life" (John 6:63).

Theodore of Mopsuestia, a master of Eastern Eucharistic tradition, wrote: "By virtue of the liturgical action, it is as if Our Lord were risen from the dead and pours his grace on all of us, through the Holy Spirit. . . . When the priest declares that the bread and wine are the Body and Blood of Christ, he affirms that this has come about through the Holy Spirit. It is the same as what happened to Christ's natural body when it received the Holy Spirit and his unction. At the moment the Holy Spirit comes, we believe that the bread and wine receive a special unction of grace. And from then on we believe they are the Body and Blood of Christ, immortal, incorruptible, impassible and immutable by nature, like the Body of Christ at the resurrection."[7]

However, we must not lose sight of the fact that the Holy Spirit does not act independently of Jesus; he acts within his words. Jesus says of the Spirit: "He will not speak on his own authority, but whatever he hears he will speak. . . . He will glorify me, for he will take what is mine and declare it to you" (John 16:13-14). That is why we must not separate, much less contrast, the words of Jesus ("This is my Body") from the epiclesis ("May the Holy Spirit make this bread into the Body of Christ"). The call to unity, for both Catholic and Orthodox faithful, springs from the very heart of the Eucharistic mystery. Even if, for obvious reasons, the memorial of the institution and the invocation to the Holy Spirit take place at two distinct moments (mortals cannot express the mystery at just one instant), their action is, nevertheless, simultaneous. Its effectiveness undoubtedly comes from the Spirit (and not from the priest or the Church), but it works within and through Christ's words. St. Ambrose exclaimed: "Do you see the effectiveness of Christ's words?"[8] Now we know where this effectiveness comes from: from the Holy Spirit! Jesus says: "This is my Body," as if he were saying: I want this bread to be my Body! And the Holy Spirit fulfills the will of Jesus each time. This is then how that marvellous "collaboration" I have mentioned is fulfilled: at the consecration the Holy Spirit gives us Jesus so that at communion, Jesus can give us the Holy Spirit.

I have said that the effectiveness that makes Jesus present on the altar does not spring from the Church but neither does it take place without the Church. The Church is the living channel through which and with which the Holy Spirit acts. It is the same for the coming of Jesus on the altar as it will be for the final coming in glory: *The Spirit and the Bride* (the Church) *say* to Jesus: *Come!* (cf. Rev 22:17). And he comes.

5. *The importance of faith: Protestant spirituality*

The Roman tradition highlights "who" is present in the Eucharist, Christ; the Orthodox tradition highlights "by whom" this presence is effected, the Holy Spirit; Protestant theology highlights "on whom" this presence is effective; in other words, the conditions that make the sacrament really effective in those that receive it. The conditions are many but they can be summed up under one heading: faith.

Let us not concern ourselves immediately and exclusively with the negative aspects which have been criticized at certain times in the Protestant principle that the sacraments are only "signs of faith." Let us forget misunderstandings and controversies and we shall find that this energetic recall to faith is beneficial to saving the sacrament and preventing it from becoming (as happened in Luther's time and others) just another "good work," or something that works mechanically or magically as it were, almost without human knowledge. In the end, it is a question of discovering the profound meaning of the exclamation that re-echoes in the liturgy at the end of the consecration and which was once placed at the center of the consecration formula, as if to emphasize that faith is intrinsic to the mystery: "Mysterium fidei," mystery of faith!

Faith doesn't "make" the sacrament but it "receives" it. Only Christ's words repeated by the Church and rendered effective by the Holy Spirit "make" the sacrament. But what would a sacrament "made" and not received avail? Concerning the incarnation, men like Origen, St. Augustine and St. Bernard said: "What advantage is it to me that Christ was born of Mary in Bethlehem if he is not born through faith in my heart too?" We can say the same of the Eucharist; what advantage is it to me that Christ is really present on the altar, if to me he is not present? A transmitting radio station would be of no use to anyone if there were no receiving sets to pick up the waves. Music exists only where there is an ear to hear it. Faith was necessary even when Jesus was physically present on this earth; otherwise — as he himself repeated many times in the gospel — his presence was of no use, if not to condemn: "Woe to you Chorazin, woe to you Capernaum!" (Matt 11:21f.).

Faith is essential to make the presence of Jesus in the Eucharist not just "real" but "personal," a one-to-one presence. "Being there" is one thing, "being present" another. Presence presupposes someone present to someone else; it presupposes reciprocal communication, an exchange between two free persons who are aware of and open to each other. There is much more involved, therefore, than simply staying in a given place.

Such a subjective and existential dimension of the Eucharistic presence does not annul the objective presence that precedes human faith, it actually presupposes it and gives it value. Luther, who raised the role of faith to such heights, was also one of the staunchest defenders of the doctrine of Christ's real presence in the Eucharist. In the course of a debate on the subject with other Reformers, he never tired of constantly repeating these same concepts, in different words: "I cannot interpret the words 'This is my Body' differently from how they sound. It is up to others, therefore, to prove that, where the words 'This is my Body' are said, Christ's Body is not present. I do not want to hear explanations based on reason. In front of such clear words, there can be no question; I refuse logical reasoning and plain common sense. I totally refuse practical demonstrations and analytical argumenta-

86

tion. God is above all kinds of mathematical certainties and we must adore the Word of God in wonder."[9]

This quick look at the wealth of riches contained in the various Christian traditions is sufficient to see the immense gift that unfolds for the Church when the various Christian denominations accept to unite their spiritual assets, as the first Christians did, who "had all things in common" (Acts 2:44). It is the same as for the rebuilding of the Temple in the prophet Haggai's time. The Israelites were all busy rebuilding and adorning their own houses when God spoke to them through his prophet: "Is it a time for yourselves to dwell in your panelled houses, while this house lies in ruins?" (Hag 1:4). Then the people took wood up to the hills and built the house and God was pleased and manifested his glory.

I feel that God is saying again today to Christians: Is it a time for yourselves to dwell in your "Churches," while my Son's body is still divided? St. Paul attributed the weakness of the Corinth community to two factors: to eating the Lord's supper in an "unworthy manner" (therefore, their bad conduct) and to eating it "separately" (therefore, their divisions). In fact, there were some that consumed their own meals, content to have the food they themselves needed with them, and completely ignored the others (cf. 1 Cor 11:20ff.). We must listen to the warning this holds for us and learn to "wait" for each other at the Lord's meal and each one share the treasures of one's own tradition with the others and not believe we possess everything, despising what others possess. This is the true *agape,* encompassing the whole Church, which the Lord makes us want to see realized, for the glory of our common Father and the good of his Church.

6. *The sentiment of the presence*

We have now terminated our little Eucharistic pilgrimage through the different Christian denominations. We have collected a few baskets of crumbs from the big multiplication of bread in the Church. But we cannot conclude here our reflections on the mystery of the real presence. It would be like collecting the crumbs and not eating them. Faith in the real presence is a wonderful thing, but it is not enough; at least, faith taken in a certain way is not enough. It is not enough to have an exact, profound and theologically perfect idea of Christ's real presence in the Eucharist.

Many theologians know all about the mystery: from the disputes in Berengar's time to modern times on the transubstantiation and transignification, yet they do not know the real presence. In biblical terms you "know" something only when you have experienced it. To know fire, you would have to have been, at least once, so close to a flame to risk being burnt.

St. Gregory of Nyssa left us an amazingly profound expression of this higher kind of faith; he speaks of a "sentiment of the presence (*aisthesis parousias*)"[10] a person experiences when seized by God's presence and has a certain perception (not just an idea) that God is there. This is not a natural perception; it is the fruit of grace. There is a strong analogy between this and what happened when, after his resurrection, Jesus appeared to someone. It was something sudden that unexpectedly and absolutely changed the person's state of mind. On Easter morning, Jesus appeared to Mary and said to her: "Woman, why are you weeping?" But she supposed him to be the gardener. Nothing has happened yet; it is a normal conversation between two people. But then Jesus calls her by name: *Mary!* and immediately the veil is removed: *"Rabbouni!"* It is you, Master! (John 21:11ff.). A few days later, the apostles were fishing in the lake; a man stood on the beach. He started talking from a distance: "Children, have you any fish?" and they answered him, "No!" But then, in a flash of understanding, John cried out: "It is the Lord!" Everything is different after this recognition and everybody hurries ashore (cf. John 21:4f.). The same thing happened, even if in a quieter way, to the disciples of Emmaus. Jesus was walking with them, "but their eyes were kept from recognizing him"; finally, when he broke the bread, "their eyes were opened and they recognized him" (Luke 24:13ff.).

The same thing happens when a Christian, who has received Jesus in the Eucharist numerous times, one day, finally, through grace, "recognizes" him and understands the truth contained in the words: "Behold, something greater than Solomon is here." It was an experience like this that gave life to the charismatic renewal in the Catholic Church. Some young American Catholics were spending a weekend in a retreat house when, one evening, in chapel, before the Most Holy Sacrament, a strange thing happened. One of them later described it in these terms: "Fear of the Lord welled up within us; a fearful awe kept us from looking up. He was personally present and we feared being loved too much. We worshipped him, knowing for the first time the meaning of worship. We knew a burning experience of the terrible reality and presence of the Lord that has since caused us to understand at first hand the images of Yahweh on Mt. Sinai as it rumbles and explodes with the fire of his Being, and the experience of Isaiah 6:1-5, and the statement that our God is a consuming fire. This holy fear was somehow the same as love or evoked love as we really beheld him. He was altogether lovely and beautiful, yet we saw no visual image. It was as though the splendorous, brilliant, personal God had come into the room and filled both it and us."[11]

7. *Our answer to the mystery of the real presence*

From faith and the "sentiment" of the real presence, reverence must spring spontaneously, and, indeed, a sense of tenderness for Jesus in the Sacrament. This is such a delicate and personal sentiment that words might even destroy it. St. Francis of Assisi, who has often been our master in Eucharistic devotion in these reflections, has something to tell us at this point. His heart overflowed with the sentiments of reverence and tenderness. In his letter "To all clerics on reverence for Christ's Body," he wrote sorrowfully: "Those who are in charge of these sacred mysteries, and especially those who are careless about their task, should realize that the chalices, corporals and altar linens where the Body and Blood of our Lord Jesus Christ are offered in sacrifice should be completely suitable. And besides, many clerics reserve the Blessed Sacrament in unsuitable places, or carry It about irreverently, or receive It unworthily, or give It to all-comers without distinction. . . . Surely we cannot be left unmoved by loving sorrow for all this; in his love, God gives himself into our hands; we touch him and receive him daily into our mouths. Have we forgotten that we must fall into his hands? And so we must correct these and all other abuses."[12]

St. Francis was overcome with pity before Jesus in the Sacrament, just as he was moved before the Child in Bethlehem. He saw him so helpless, so entrusted to humanity; especially so humble. To him, he was always the same Jesus, living and real, never a theological abstraction. "It affects me like this," he wrote in his *Testament,* "because in this world I cannot see the most high Son of God with my own eyes, except for his most holy Body and Blood."[13]

The Eucharist is the biggest of the Church's responsibilities in history. The Church is responsible for many things: sound doctrine, humanity, culture, treasures of art. But these are small responsibilities compared to that concerning the Saviour's Body and Blood which are the price of our ransom.

Once, at the beginning of Christianity, the so-called "Discipline of the Secret" (*Disciplina arcani*) was in force. The Eucharist could not be spoken of thoughtlessly or lightly, much less shown indiscriminately to everyone. Even converts were only fully introduced to the Eucharistic mystery in the week following their baptism: as neophytes and not as catechumens. It was a moment they awaited anxiously because of the secrecy that surrounded it. Today, we wonder why so many precautions were taken. Was it simply fear of derision and profanation by the pagans? This fear did exist but, at heart, it was really a sign of veneration and religious wonder before such closeness on God's part. "Arcane" derives from *arcere* which means to keep far off, to hide, to protect from profane eyes. For this reason, on inscriptions and in paintings, the Eucharist was hidden from pagans beneath the fish symbol and other symbols. Perhaps the time has come to restore the arcane discipline. Not in the form but in the spirit. And not so much because of the danger of the Eucharist being profaned (unfortunately, this danger exists too) as that it might be made commonplace, just an "ordinary" thing to be treated with familiarity and superficiality. Priests ought to remind themselves of this first of all, for they are the ones who handle the Body and Blood of Christ daily, they are the "guardians" charged by the Church and the most likely to become inured and to forget that they are handling God and God is to be adored. With God, reverence must always accompany familiarity.

People receive their first catechesis on the Eucharist from the way a parish priest behaves at the altar and from how he passes in front of the Most Holy Sacrament. A certain way of genuflecting before the tabernacle can say more than a whole sermon on the real presence. There are many little signs that indicate how deeply the presence of Jesus is felt in a Christian community: clean altar cloths, a fresh flower (one maybe, but fresh), a well-tended lamp. We must not be hasty to scorn exterior signs. If God's

Son did not disdain to show his love for us through signs, like the Eucharistic signs, why should we fear to show him our love with visible signs? It is true that Jesus delights in the sentiments of the heart and not in gestures, but we need gestures to move and express the sentiments of the heart. The care and delicacy (not affectation) given to the Blessed Sacrament in a church is a thermometer for measuring the level of faith and devotion in the priest and the community which gather there.

A nonbeliever in the real presence said: "If I could believe that God is really there on the altar, I think I would fall on my knees and stay there forever." Jesus is probably not demanding this of us, because we also have duties to charity and service to our brothers and sisters. He is probably not asking us to stay kneeling physically, but spiritually he is asking us to do so. In our hearts we can stay in adoration of the Blessed Sacrament while our hands are working, writing, absolving. A Christian's life, particularly where religious and priests are concerned, must be oriented to the tabernacle. By an ancient tradition, churches have always been "oriented," that is, they look towards the "Orient," because it was in Jerusalem, in the Orient, that Christ died and rose again. So the temple of our hearts must look towards the Orient, towards the Sun of justice shining on the Church from the Eucharist. Jesus said that where our treasure is, there will our hearts be also (cf. Matt 6:21). Our greatest treasure in this world ("the treasure hidden in the field") is Jesus in the Eucharist, and none other. May our hearts be there, may they return there after our night's rest, may their dwelling place be the tabernacle. It is possible to spend, in spirit, hours and hours on our knees before the Most Holy Sacrament while still working or traveling.

It is important to cultivate interior silence, to be present to the present. Presence, we have seen, presupposes another presence. Instead, we are absent more often than not. If, according to one of the possible interpretations of Exodus 3:14, God is "He who is there," the human being he who "is not there," who lives outside himself, alienated, "abroad." Thinking back to the time of his conversion, St. Augustine sadly exclaimed: "You were with me, but I was not with you!"[14] To meet Jesus in the sacrament, it is necessary first of all to pass from outside to inside, from the exterior to the interior.

When the disciples of Emmaus "recognized" the Lord as he broke the bread, they no longer cared that "it was toward evening'' and hastened to Jerusalem to tell the other disciples. He who really recognizes the Lord in the Eucharist, spontaneously becomes an apostle of the real presence. Faith leads to experience and experience to witnessing. John the Baptist is the unequalled witness of how to preach the mystery of the real presence. Not with many words but simply ''in Spirit and power,'' crying: ''Among you stands one whom you do not know!'' (John 1:26). He ''points'' the way in a precise direction saying: ''Behold, the Lamb of God!'' and the disciples heard him and left him to follow the Lamb (cf. John 1:35ff.). We have reflected on the real presence of Jesus among us; let us remember that this presence is not only a gift, but, as I have said, a responsibility too. That day Jesus said: ''The queen of the South will arise at the judgment with this generation and condemn it; for she came from the ends of the earth to hear the wisdom of Solomon and behold, something greater than Solomon is here!''

NOTES

1. St. Thomas Aquinas, *Theological Summa,* III, q. 60, a. 3.
2. Hymn *O sacrum Convivium.*
3. St. Ambrose, *On the Sacraments,* IV, 14–16 (PL 16, 439f.).
4. Cf. Denzinger–Schönmetzer, *Enchiridion Symbolorum,* nr. 690.
5. St. Thomas Aquinas, *Theological Summa,* III, q. 75, a. 4.
6. Hymn *Lauda Sion.*
7. Theodore of Mopsuestia, *Catecheses,* XVI, 11f. (Studi e Testi 145, Roma 1949) 551f.
8. St. Ambrose, *On the Sacraments,* IV, 14–16 (PL 16, 439).
9. M. Luther at the Colloquy of Marburg in the year 1529 (Weimar ed., 30, 3, pp. 110f.).
10. St. Gregory of Nyssa, *On the Canticle,* XI, 5, 2 (PG 44, 1001).
11. R. Martin (ed.), *The Spirit and the Church,* New York 1976, 16.
12. St. Francis of Assisi, *Writings,* 101.
13. St. Francis of Assisi, *Testament (Writings,* 67).
14. St. Augustine, *Confessions,* X, 27.

Chapter Eight

"Until He Comes"

The Eucharist as waiting for the Lord's coming

"As often as you eat this bread and drink this cup, you proclaim the Lord's death until he comes" (1 Cor 11:26). These words of the apostle re-echo at every Mass; in fact, after the consecration we exclaim: "We proclaim your death, Lord Jesus, until you come in glory!" It is an echo of the *Maranatha,* of the "Come Lord!" (or "The Lord comes!") which was part of the Eucharistic celebration in the early days of the Church. St. Jerome spoke of "an apostolic tradition" in use up to his time, according to which the people could not be dismissed before midnight at the Easter Vigil, because the parousia of the Lord could well take place up to then.[1] This demonstrates how real and alive was the expectation of Christ's return in the Church's primitive liturgy.

1. *"Sursum corda!"*

The waiting and longing for the Lord's return, the so-called eschatological tension, is not a purely subjective fact that exists only in the minds of those who attend the rite, but it has its roots in the depth of the mystery and is intrinsic to Eucharistic celebration.

In the Jewish Passover there was a sense of waiting for something, even if this too was in "figure." They had to eat the lamb with their "loins girded, sandals on their feet, a staff in their hands and in haste" (cf. Exod 12:11), as if about to leave. The very name "Passover" (*Pascha*) implied "passage" or "emigration," for, according to many authors it indicated the coming out of Egypt into the Promised Land, from this world to the Father. Now, in the Eucharist, the haste has become more spiritual, more profound. It is the very way in which Jesus is present in the sacrament that makes us long for his coming. It's a "veiled" presence, as it were, a presence-absence. God reveals himself in the Eucharist, just as he did in the incarnation, by veiling himself lest his creatures be destroyed by the radiance of his majesty. And it is because he is hidden that we long to see him "without veils." Those that love him know this as did the author of the "Adoro te devote":

> "Jesus! Whom for the present veiled I see,
> What I so thirst for, oh, vouchsafe to me:
> That I may see thy countenance unfolding,
> And may be blest thy glory in beholding."

A hidden and partial presence is not sufficient for those that love. In "The Canticle of the soul consumed with the desire to see God" St. John of the Cross uses these words for the Eucharist, no doubt fruit of his experience:

> "When to temper the pangs
> I gaze on you in the Sacrament,
> The veil that conceals you
> increases my torment.
> I am a prey to agony
> while I dwell here below
> I die because I do not die."

Instead of quenching our thirst for God's presence, the Eucharist increases it and makes it a stronger torment. St. Paul says the same thing with the image of the "first fruits." We have the first fruits of the Spirit, but in this having we realize that the first fruits are not enough for us; the first fruits make us long for the whole crop, they make us long for the whole. And so, adds the apostle: "We groan inwardly as we wait for adoption as sons, the redemption of our bodies" (Rom 8:23).

In this way the Eucharist reveals the condition of the Christian existence on this earth. It is a moment of privilege in which the Church experiences herself as a "pilgrim" Church. It is the *viaticum* "the bread of travelers," a continuation of the Exodus, the paschal sacrament, and that is, of "passage." From the very beginning of the Church the cry "Sursum corda!," "Lift up your hearts," has been echoing in the introduction to the preface of the Mass. And St. Augustine commented: "The entire life of true Christians is an endless 'sursum cor.' What does it mean to have our hearts 'lifted up'? It means to have hope in God. When you hear the priest say: 'Sursum corda!,' you answer: 'Habemus ad Dominum,' we have them lifted up to the Lord! Make sure that what you answer is true."[2] Many of the Fathers of the Church, referring to Hebrews 10:1, distinguished three stages, or times, in the history of salvation: the time of *shadow,* of *image* and of *reality:* "The shadow is in the Law, the image in the Gospel, but reality is in heaven. Now we are walking in the image; when the fullness of perfection comes, we shall see it face to face, because perfection is in the reality."[3] Consequently, the Fathers then distinguished three Passovers: the Passover of the Law, that of the gospel and "a third Passover that will be fulfilled amidst myriads of angels at the supreme feast and blessed exodus to heaven."[4] Jesus himself had launched the idea of a "heavenly Passover" when, at the institution of the Eucharist, he spoke of a mysterious new Passover to be fulfilled in "the kingdom of God" (cf. Luke 22:16).

2. *The Eucharist makes the Parish*

The Eucharist therefore encourages us to live eschatologically, as pilgrims, with our eyes and hearts lifted up to God. In the preceding chapters, I showed how the Eucharist makes the Church; now, in this final reflection, let us see how the Eucharist makes the parish!

What is a parish? I myself was surprised to discover that the Bible talks amply about "parishes" and "parish priests" — terms that come from *paraoikeo,* which, in its turn, occurs frequently in both the Old Testament and the Greek New Testament. It is, therefore, to the Bible that we turn to find out what exactly a parish is or what it should be.

The Acts of the Apostles tell us that Israel was "in exile in the land of Egypt" (Acts 13:17). Where modern translations use the word "exile," the original Greek text uses "parish" (*paroikia*). Elsewhere, we are told that Abraham, by faith, lived a "parochial" life, or, as it is translated, as an alien and exile (cf. 15:13; Heb 11:9). Let us now come to Christians, to the new Israel. In his First Letter, Peter warns us: "Conduct yourselves with fear throughout the time of your exile" (1 Pet 1:17); literally this means: "in the time of your parochial life." Immediately afterwards he says: "I beseech you as aliens and exiles to abstain from the passions of the flesh" (1 Pet 2:11); again taken literally, it means: "I beseech you as parishioners."

What do these curious expressions mean and what do *paroikia* and *paroikos* mean? It is quite simple: *para* is an adverb and means beside; *oikia* is a noun and means house, dwelling-place. We have, therefore: dwelling beside and not within. The term further indicates someone sojourning in a given place for a short time, someone passing through, or in exile; *paroikia* therefore indicates a *temporary* dwelling-place. To the meaning of temporariness is added that of *precariousness*. In fact, aliens do not have the same rights as citizens. Parishioners (*paroikoi*), then, in contrast to citizens with full rights, also indicates aliens. If a war were to break out between his native place and the place of adoption, the alien knows he would feel the consequences, unless he were to deny his homeland.

Why, then, does the Bible define Christian life as one of "parishioners," and that is, as pilgrims and aliens? The clear answer is because Christians are "in" the world but not "of" the world (cf. John 17:10, 16); for their real commonwealth is in heaven, from where they await a Saviour, the Lord Jesus Christ (cf. Phil 3:20); for here they have no lasting city, but seek the city that is to come (cf. Heb 13:14). In this general sense, the whole Church is one big "parish." At the beginning this was the basic self-consciousness of the Christian community. It is expressed in the letters exchanged by the first communities. The well-known letter of St. Clement Pope to the Corinthian Church, opened with these words: "God's Church which is alien (literally, lives its parochial life) in Rome, to God's Church, alien in Corinth."[5] The Christians of Smyrna announced the martyrdom of St. Polycarp to the Christians in another town with these words: "God's Church that is alien (*paroikousa*) at Smyrna, to God's Church, alien in Filomelo."[6] Diognetus's Epistle — a very ancient document — defines a Christian as one who "lives as an alien (*paroikos*) in a homeland, who participates in everything like a citizen but bears with everything like a pilgrim; one for whom every foreign land is a homeland and every homeland a foreign land."[7]

This reminds me that in today's diplomatic language, the Vatican defines itself as a "foreign state" and the pope as the "head of a foreign state." This has one meaning for "those outside" but for us believers it should have a much more radical meaning. The Vatican, as the representative and center of the Catholic Church, is a "foreign" state, not only for Italy and any other existing state, but for the whole world. It is, in fact, the state of a people who are foreigners and pilgrims in this world!

However, this is a special way of being a stranger in the world. Certain doctrines have instilled in mortals a sense of alienation and escape from the world. In different ways, Platonics and Gnostics defined the human being as being "by nature, an alien in this world." Yet there is a great difference: they held that the world was a work of evil and therefore humans should not commit themselves to it through marriage, work or the state. This does not appertain to Christians. A Christian "marries and has children," and "participates in everything."[8] Such is an eschatological, and not an ontological, alienation; Christians are alien by vocation and not by nature, in so far that they are destined for another world and not that they come from another world. The Christian sentiment of alienation is based on Christ's resurrection: "If you had been raised with Christ, seek the things that are above" (Col 3:1). It does not, therefore, deny creation and its fundamental beauty and good.

In the Bible the parish concept is integrated with "diaspora," or dispersion: "Peter, an apostle of Jesus Christ, to the exiles of the dispersion . . ." (1 Pet 1:1). Diaspora means dissemination. Christians are God's seeds scattered all over the world so that the world may become God's field full of good fruit. They have no hostility or contempt for the world; it is God's and God "loves the world" and wants "to save the world" (cf. John 3:16; 12:47). It is true that Christians must also be the "salt of the earth," and they can only be so if, even while being dissolved into the world, they never lose their "taste," their otherness to the world; if they know how to introduce the germ of eternity and incorruption into this world of ours that is held in the grip of temporariness and corruption. In other words, Christians are the "salt of the earth," when they live as pilgrims and exiles in this world.

They say that Christian wisdom consists in a balance between transcendence and immanence. It is often seen in the way of dosage — a little bit of transcendence and a bit of immanence, a bit of attention for the "next" world and a bit for "this" world, without exaggerating on either side. But this is a human and carnal

97

way of reasoning. Where God is concerned, balance is never the result of measuring opposites; it is the powerful simultaneous presence of opposites. We must "exaggerate," going the whole way in one sense and the other. This creates the "wonderful paradox of Christian life."[9] The paschal mystery does not consist in preaching a bit about the Cross and a bit about the resurrection, but in accepting all the implications of the Cross so as to fully relish the resurrection. Thus, Christian wisdom consists in using this world as if it were to pass tomorrow and working for this world as if it were never going to pass.

3. *"Behold, the Bridegroom!"*

We begin now to see how and why the Eucharist makes the parish. It does so because it keeps Christians with their "loins girded, a staff in their hand and sandals on their feet," in a permanent state of exodus, and because, through the daily reminder of Mass it prevents the Church from falling into a rut, "installed" and ready to sit back, a Church in slumber. The world needs parishes that are places of pilgrimage and joy and not centers that offer all kinds of services, activities and entertainments. The world itself creates and diffuses these things and is even bored with them. It needs a place where the presence of the Spirit can be felt. Those approaching a parish for the first time should be able to feel that it is different and like the new members of the first Christian communities, be moved to say: "God is really among you!" (1 Cor 14:25).

Sadly, with the passing of time, much of the original meaning of parish has been lost, so much so, that we skim through the pages of the Bible without even recognizing it. The term parish has been reduced to simply mean the subdivision of a diocese, an administrative unit of the local Church. Consequently, parishioner has come to mean "pertaining to a parish," with no reference whatever to the idea of pilgrim and exile.

In more recent times, the new emphasis on the role and commitment of Christians in the affairs of the world has helped to minimize further the eschatological sense of Christian life. We, too, like the foolish maidens, consider that night is made for sleep. It is exactly what happened in the parable: "As the bridegroom was delayed, they all slumbered and slept" (Matt 25:5).

98

But, lo, a cry pierces the deep slumber the world has fallen into: "Wise maidens, trim your lamps: Behold, the bridegroom!" Just as once the sentinels signalled from one tower to another that the king was approaching, so this cry must run throughout the whole Church and shake it. Behold, the bridegroom! He is coming! He said he would come and he will. "His coming is sure as the dawn" (Hos 6:3). The Lord has filled my heart with a cry I cannot contain; I feel it surging in me and sweeping me along like a maelstrom. Wherever I go to preach these days, I am forced to cry out with all my strength: My brothers and sisters, it is time to wake up! "The end of all things is at hand" (1 Pet 4:7); "The judge is standing at the doors" (Jas 5:9). I repeat the words of the psalm of exile to myself: "Let my tongue cleave to the roof of my mouth, if I do not remember you; if I forget you, O Jerusalem; if I do not set Jerusalem — the heavenly Jerusalem — above my every thought and above everything I preach" (cf. Ps 137:5ff.).

It is all too easy to hide behind the excuse that "this is apocalyptic preaching, on the end of the world!" It's not apocalyptic preaching; it is eschatological preaching, or simply, Christian preaching. The difference is that *in apocalyptic preaching* what counts is "when" Christ will come, the day and hour, and that's what periodically gives rise to the previsions of false prophets on the imminent end of the world, whereas Jesus cut short such speculations when he said that no one knows of the day and the hour and that it is not for us to know times or seasons which the Father has fixed on his own authority (cf. Matt 24:36; Acts 1:7). In *eschatological preaching* instead, what counts is "that" he will come, that there will be an end, that "the form of this world is passing away" (cf. 1 Cor 7:31). Should this make the question less serious and urgent? How foolish we would be to console ourselves with the thought that after all no one knows when the end will come! As if the end could not be tomorrow, or even tonight, for me. It would be the Lord's coming for me, nothing more and nothing less. In Revelation Jesus says: "I am coming soon" (Rev 22:20) and he knows what he says!

The bishop and martyr, St. Cyprian, said to the Christians of Carthage: "My dear brethren, God's kingdom is at hand; the reward of life, the bliss of eternal salvation, everlasting happiness and the possession of paradise, which we once lost, are coming again with the passing of this world; the things of heaven are about to follow the things of earth, great things will follow small things and eternal things will follow what is passing.''[10] Who could say that St. Cyprian was deceiving himself or his people that day just because many centuries have passed since then and nothing has happened? What he said was true for each one of them at the right time, and blessed are those that really listened to him!

To understand the language of the Bible and the Fathers on this point, we must keep this fact in mind. When we talk today of the end of the world we are thinking, according to our modern culture, of the absolute end, after which there can only be eternity. The Bible reasons more realistically and in relative categories. When therefore it mentions the end of the world, it very often meant the actual world that exists for a certain group of people as they know it: "their" world. It is more a question of the end of "a" world than "the" world. So it is not true at all that all the previsions on the end of the world have been belied by events. Jesus said: "This generation will not pass. . . ." (Matt 24:34), and events proved him right: that generation had not passed before the "Jewish world" ended tragically with the destruction of Jerusalem. Also the Roman world ended with the barbarians. And when Rome was sacked in A.D. 410 and the Fathers thought it was the end of the world, they were not mistaken in substance; one world really did end and another began. Likewise, a world ended with the rise of Communism in certain Eastern countries and still another world has ended with its fall . . . . And who can tell us if, today, the world we have built ourselves, drugging it with progress and quiet rebellion against God, is not about to end amidst all the confusion and unsettlement that these historical changes cause? What Jesus said still remains true: "You must be ready; for the Son of man is coming at an hour you do not expect" (Matt 24:44).

4. *Waiting and commitment*

The source of Christian hope is to be found in these words of a song: "The Lord is coming, trials will soon be over." St. Paul actually calls it blessed hope: "Let us live, he says, awaiting our blessed hope, the appearing of the glory of our great God and Saviour Jesus Christ" (cf. Titus 2:13). This is the only great truth that moves all and towards which all moves; it is the only really important news that faith has to offer the world: the Lord is coming! Let us try to imagine what life, the world, faith itself, would be without this surety: everything would be obscure and absurd. If we have hoped in Christ for this life only, we are of all people most to be pitied (cf. 1 Cor 15:19). In ancient times they used to say that a thing was known by its end (for them, "finis" signified both aim and end). Therefore, he who is not aware of where he is going and where he tends, does not even really know this world. One who is not aware that he or she is going towards the coming Lord is playing with history and misunderstands it.

The proclamation of the Lord's coming is the strength of Christian preaching. Why be silent then, why keep this light that could set fire to the world, under a bushel? I believe that God's command to the prophet Isaiah is addressed to the entire Church: "Get you up to a high mountain, lift up your voice, fear not; say to the cities of Judah, 'Behold, the Lord God comes with might'" (Is 40:9ff.).

To renounce proclaiming the end of the world for fear of alarming the world is the same as repeating, on a wider scale, the foolishness of those families that refuse to inform a relative of approaching death for fear of causing distress; this will certainly not prevent the person from dying but it might prevent him or her from dying well. "What kind of love do we have for Jesus Christ," St. Augustine exclaimed, "if we fear his coming? Are we not ashamed, brethren? We love him and yet fear his coming? Do we really love him then? Or do we not, perhaps, love our sins more than Christ?"[11]

It is our pressing duty to restore to the faithful a sense of familiarity, of nostalgia for the heavenly homeland and, why not, for Paradise. They have gradually been deprived of these things by careless teachers who have fallen prey to certain atheistic ideologies which see "the other world" only in terms of alienation. A genuine biblical expectation of the Lord's coming does not detract from neighborly zeal but actually purifies it. It teaches us to "wisely use the goods of this world, keeping in mind the goods of heaven," as an Advent liturgical prayer tells us. St. Paul, after reminding Christians that "time is short," concluded, saying: "So then, as we have opportunity, let us do good to all people, and especially to those who are of the household of faith!" (cf. Gal 6:10). Even Jesus taught us that while we await his return, we should wash each other's feet. If our Eucharist is eschatological, it is also true that our eschatology is Eucharistic, or made up of service and self-donation until death.

To live waiting and longing for the Lord's return does not mean to desire an early death. These sentiments have nothing to do with the eschatological tension. There are some that wish to be free of the body to be with Christ, others desire a long life in the flesh to serve the Lord and others who love to say with St Paul: "Yet which I shall choose I cannot tell" (Phil 1:22), and this is the best solution. In this, each one has his or her own gift. To "seek the things of heaven," means to orientate our life to meeting the Lord, to make this the pole of attraction and beacon of our life. Here again "when" is of secondary importance and we must serenely leave it in God's hands.

5. *"Let us go to the House of the Lord!"*

The time of waiting for Christ to come again is not therefore to be considered a negative time lived in disgust with the world and life. There is every reason for living it positively — a longing for the true life we will have when Jesus comes again. Church liturgy has always called the day of a saint's death a "birth-day" (*dies natalis*). Jesus speaks of "travail" (cf. John 16:21) and, indeed, it will really be like a passage from the dark womb of this visible world and a leap into the light of full truth.

It is not, therefore, a message of sadness and fear but one of joy and hope. The Hebrew Psalter contains a group of psalms called the "psalms of ascensions," or "canticles of Zion." These were psalms sung by Israelite pilgrims as they "climbed" towards the Holy City on pilgrimage. One of them begins like this: "I was glad when they said to me, 'Let us go to the house of the Lord!'" (Ps 122:1). These psalms have now become the psalms of the pilgrim Church on the way to the heavenly Jerusalem; our psalms. When commenting on the opening words of the psalm just mentioned, St. Augustine said to those listening: "Think, brethren, of what happens when the people are told of a martyr's feast, or a gathering place is fixed to celebrate the feastday; how excited the people become and they encourage one another to go! If asked where they are going, they will reply: There, to that place, that sanctuary! They go on talking like this and, as it were, inflaming one another, and so they form one flame, each communicating to the other the flame that is burning in himself and making them all come together in that holy place. If then pure love can transport the faithful to a simple sanctuary, how much more sublime should the love of those be, who, living in concord, can say to each other: 'Let us go to the house of the Lord!' Well, then, let us run! Let us make haste for we are going to the Lord's house; let us hasten for the race will not tire us; for we shall reach a place where there is no weariness. Let us go to the Lord's house and our hearts will rejoice with those who tell us to do so. They saw the homeland before us and as we follow them, in the distance they cry to us: 'Let us go to the house of the Lord!' Hasten, run! The apostles saw it and told us: Run, make haste, follow us! 'Let us go to the house of the Lord!' "[12]

This is not a physical race. It is spiritual and our paces are our holy desires and the works of light. Jesus has gone before us, like the coryphaeus of the huge pilgrimage of humankind towards God, to the heavenly sanctuary. He has opened for us "a new and living way through the curtain, that is, through his flesh" (cf. Heb 10:20). We are following on footprints that have already left their mark for us — the perfume of his unguent, the Holy Spirit.

In every Eucharist, the Spirit and the Bride say (to Jesus) "Come!" (Rev 22:17). And we too who have been listening say to Jesus: Come! Maranatha!

NOTES

1. St. Jerome, *On the Gospel of Matthew,* IV, 25, 6 (CCL 77, 236f.).
2. St. Augustine, *Sermon Denis* 6 (PL 46, 834f.).
3. St. Ambrose, *On the Offices,* I, 48 (PL 16, 94).
4. Origen, *On the Gospel of John,* X, 111 (GCS, 1903, 189).
5. St Clement, *Letter to the Corinthians,* inscr. (Bihlmeyer–Schneemelcher, Tübingen 1956) 35.
6. *Martyrdom of St Polycarp,* inscr. (Bihlmeyer–Schneemelcher) 120.
7. *Epistle to Diognetus,* V, 5 (Bihlmeyer–Schneemelcher) 144.
8. Ibid., V, 5-6.
9. Ibid., V, 4.
10. St. Cyprian, *On Mortality,* 2 (CCL 3A, 17f.).
11. St. Augustine, *On the Psalms,* 95, 14 (CCL 39, 1352).
12. St. Augustine, *On the Psalms,* 121, 2 (CCL 40, 1802).